MAKING IT HAPPEN!
How to Make Dreams into a Reality

Mario J. Muthe

Making it Happen! How to Make Dreams into a Reality, 1st Edition, Copyright 2018© Mario J. Muthe.

All rights reserved. No part of this book may be reproduced or transmitted in any form whatsoever, electronic, or mechanical, including photocopying, recording, or by any informational storage or retrieval system without the expressed written, dated and signed permission from the author.

Book Cover: Kim Li
Layout Design: Laura Gibbs
Copy Editor: Jill McKellan

Printed in the United States of America

Dedication

I want to dedicate this book to my wife. Ever since the first day we were together, she has continuously given me her unconditional love and kept her faith in me. Even when I was at my lowest, even when everyone doubted me and our relationship, she stood by me. Without her, I would never have been able to achieve the level of success I have today. Thank you for everything. I love you!

Acknowledgments

First of all, I would like to thank Mr. Tom Shapiro; the man who believe in me. Throughout all my years, I am very fortunate to have met several people who have really helped me in my life. Mr. Shapiro both helped me by giving me the opportunity to work for him and by placing me in front of challenges and people that he thought could help me learn and perfect a trade. As a result, I was eventually able to start a business on my own—to provide employment opportunities to other people like what he did for me. Back then, Tom probably saw me as an investment. Others in my position may have seen only a job. For me, I saw an opportunity and it was up to me to make full use of it.

I not only learned a trade. To pursue what I have, it meant I had to learn the business part, as well. A totally different subject! Being the best at a trade or service without having any knowledge of how to turn that into a business is a hindrance. Having knowledge and not applying it leads to stagnancy. Through the right mentors and motivation, I have learned that when we start seeing things from a business prospective, a totally new picture immerges.

I also want to thank my family; my wife, my two daughters, and my son. My commitment is to always be a better father and husband to all of you. I am profoundly grateful to you all for your love and support through all of this. Because of you guys, I will never give up and continue to strive to become the best.

Finally, to Wilbert Wynnberg, a great friend and mentor who got me started on this book. I sincerely thank you.

Table of Contents

Why I Wrote This Book 1

Chapter 1 | Overcoming Fear 3

  Unfounded Fears 4

  The Price We Pay for Unfounded Fears 5

  The Cause of Unfounded Fears 6

    Programmed Fear 6
    Caring too Much What Others Think 7
    Lack of Understanding 8
    Inaction 8

  How to Overcome Fear 9

    Awareness is Key 9
    Challenge Your Fear 10

  Get Over the Fear of Failure 11

    Attain Knowledge 12
    Get the Right Advice 12
    Energy Healing Modalities 12

  A Fearless Day 14

2 | Self-Improvement 15

  Self-Knowledge is the Beginning of Self-Improvement 16

  8 Ways to Improve Your Self-Awareness 17

    1. Know your strengths and weaknesses 18
    2. Know your temperament 19
    3. Examine your personal values 21

  4. Identify your interests and passions.................................22
  5. Know your biorhythms...23
  6. Find the purpose and meaning for your existence 23
  7. Observe your mind..24
  8. Indulge yourself!..24
 Expect Improvement..25
 Arm Yourself with Self-Knowledge..26

3 | Time Management 29
 External Time 29
 Internal Time..31
 Individual Perception of Time..32
 Work and Leisure Time...34
 Punctuality..35
 Passing Time 37
 Track Your Use of Time...39
 The Realities of LIFE and Time Management..........................40
 Prioritize Your Time 41
 Important Priorities 42
 Manage Your Time with Determination...................................44

4 | Money Management 47
 Achieving Financial Freedom 48
 Establishing Financial Goals...49
 Determine Your Needs..53
 What You Need to Reach Your Goal 56
 Closing the Gap..56
 Develop a Financial Plan..57
 Overcoming the Obstacles to Your Financial Goals..................59
 Your 10-Point Personal Strategy Checklist................................62

5 | How to Start a Business ... 65

Big Companies that Started in a Garage ... 66
Analyze the Market ... 67
Why You Must Love Your Customer ... 68
Do You Really Have the Dedication and Time? ... 69
Develop a New Attitude ... 70
Make a Smooth Transition ... 71
How to Take Your Ideas from Mind to Market to Profit ... 72
To Market We Go ... 73
   Branding ... *74*
   Unique Selling Proposition ... *74*
   Identifying Your Niche Market ... *74*
   Startup Costs ... *75*
Collaboration and Cooperation Versus Competition ... 76
Short To-Do-List ... 77

6 | Leadership ... 81

What is True Leadership? ... 82
7 Reasons Why Leadership is Crucial to the Success of a Business ... 83
The Greatest Leader of All Time ... 84
8 Secrets of a Great Leadership ... 86

7 | The Power of Negotiation ... 93

The Art of Negotiation ... 95
8 Tips for Remembering Your Negotiation Skills ... 96
Make an Impact ... 102

8 | How to Live Healthy ... 105

Why Live Healthy? ... 105
   You'll Feel Better Now ... *106*
   You'll Live Better and Age Better ... *106*

7 Steps to Living a Healthy Life 107
   Step 1: Get Plenty of Sleep *107*
   Step 2: Eat Healthy Foods *108*
   Step 3: Exercise *110*
   Step 4: Meditate *111*
   Step 5: Appreciate Something! *114*
   Step 6: Create a Vibrant Social Life *114*
   Step 7: Live Your Purpose *115*
Overall Health 116

About Mario J. Muthe **117**

Contact Mario J. Muthe **118**

Why I Wrote This Book

"Entrepreneurs are simply those who understand that there's little difference between obstacle and opportunity and are able to turn both to their advantage."
— **Niccolo Machiavelli**

The list of things to help change people's lives is not exhaustive. What I share in this book has worked for me and helped to shape me and improve my life. Hopefully, it'll provide you the change you seek too.

I consider myself a very successful man, because I never forget where I came from. This is a constant reminder of how blessed I am. We are in a country with endless opportunities but sometimes, we limit ourselves to recognize what's in front of us, that which may not be helping us. For example:

- The people we spend time the most with
- Only seeing the negative side
- The environment we create in our lives
- Lacking the knowledge we require
- Not being resourceful

MAKING IT HAPPEN!

These were some of the roadblocks I faced at one point in my life. Through the experience of working for Mr. Shapiro, he helped me find ways to break through those limiting beliefs. He was always implementing new things in his company to challenge me – and anyone who accepted a good challenge – to think, grow, and seek improvement.

As a result of this, the courage and strength to do what I feel is right exists. It has been intricate in leading me to the success I've discovered in my life thus far.

People ask me about what I've done to create the life I have frequently, and I am grateful to share whatever I can to help them. This is why I thank you for picking up this book. I simply can't wait for you to get started. My philosophies in business and life are poured out into here. However, this is not just about me. If you take even a fraction of this away, I sincerely feel you will have a better life on all levels and grow in wonderful ways.

Mario J. Muthe
May 2018 (*Sarasota, Florida*)

"Success is not about how much power, money or stuff you have today. Success is how well you do what you do, when no one is watching."
— **John Paul DeJoria**

Chapter 1 | Overcoming Fear

Fear can both help and hurt you…

If a seventeen foot alligator were to cross your path and notice you, fear would serve you well, wouldn't it? Your blood pressure would instantly rise… Adrenalin would flood all your muscles… It would be really scary.

Yet, the fear you experienced could also provide you the benefit of super-human strength and the ability to run at a speed you have never run before. It would be a very good idea to do just that!

But for locals in Florida, seeing an alligator is a normal thing, because they are frequently in their back yard. My point is that we fear what's unfamiliar to us, not only wild animals, but new environments, new jobs, new crowds, new schools…

The word "fear" trips people up at times. We automatically think all fear is bad. This isn't the case. Plenty of fears are good for us. They guide us to doing the right thing in the heat of the moment. It's self-preservation, which can be a good thing.

There is one other thing aside from fear filled with concern about our safety… What? It's our subconscious mind. This is the place where our greatest challenges often thrive and it isn't always easy to recognize what's happening.

Our subconscious mind usually has many unfounded fears hidden in the depths of its intelligence. These fears are from our childhoods and even those fears programmed into us by our parents and society. The intention to restrain us from good things for our life wasn't the motivator for these actions, but they often are the result. Are you ready to do something about that?

This chapter dives into fears and the subconscious mind. Together, we'll uncover ways to overcome our UNFOUNDED fears.

Unfounded Fears

Unfounded fears are those that we develop throughout childhood and life. These are the fears that stop us from doing and being our best.

Examples of unfounded fears are fear of success, fear of failure, fear of public speaking, fear of taking a chance, fear of any normal amount of risk, and many others. Basically, an unfounded fear is any fear you have developed because of some outside stimuli the subconscious mind decided was significant and something you should fear.

This is why some people have fears you cannot relate to at all… For example: Airplanes; a lot of people won't go in a plane because of the fear of altitude. Darkness; people won't go outside at night because of the fear of darkness. Deep water; a lot people won't go in a boat because of the fear of deep water, coupled with the fear of having a panic attack in public. These examples may seem trivial to someone who has never experienced them, but to those who are afflicted by them it is a very real fear. Often times, it's crippling.

But unfounded fears are not limited to only these types of examples. Most of us are affected by some type of unfounded fear. The biggest known is about public speaking. This is rated number one of all fears, whereas dying comes in at fifth. Does that give you an idea of how real this fear is for many? Let that soak in! Most people are more afraid of making a fool of themselves in public than they are of death!

Just avoiding these fears may feel like self-preservation, but it does come with a cost. What do you think you may have lost out on because of your fears?

The Price We Pay for Unfounded Fears

If you have the fear of public speaking, think of how that fear may have affected your life. The late and great Dr. Wayne Dyer used to say, "Don't die with your music still in you." It's a great reminder about fear's paralyzing impact on your life. Back to the public speaking example, if it is stopping you from singing your own song to the world, then you could not experience the opportunity to live your purpose—to let your version of music out into the world. Plus, many high-paying careers require a person to do public speaking. Are you going to live less than you could just because you let a fear hold you back? I sure hope not! Don't be one of the smart, capable people out there who may have had a major impact on the world if they could have gotten over the unfounded fear of public speaking.

This is a major example, but the "fear factor" doesn't just end with public speaking.

- If a person is afraid to ask for a raise at their job, they suffer.
- If someone is afraid to ask out someone on a date, that one special person may slip away and they will suffer.
- Or, if you have a great business idea but have an unfounded fear of failure – or success – then either of these unfounded fears may cause you to sabotage your efforts.

Fear and needless suffering go hand-in-hand. They also have a direct, major impact on most peoples' lives. The price you pay is a costly one too, a heavy burden on your heart and sense of purpose. Accepting unfounded fears can hurt your relationships, work, and business. Doesn't sound very happy or rewarding, does it? Ask yourself: why give into these fears and risk such unhappiness with yourself?

Giving in to fear can even cause you to feel depressed and can lead to a lack of self-confidence.

No doubt about it, the price we pay for our unfounded fears is truly profound. How did these fears even creep into our lives, anyway?

The Cause of Unfounded Fears

The discovery of your unfounded fears is an important one. They can arrive in a person's life for many reasons, some they consciously know about and others are deeply ingrained in their subconscious mind. Either way, unaddressed fears can create significant challenges and hindrances in your life. Don't let them rule you—take control!

Programmed Fear

Programmed fear is fear that we don't even realize was given to us by an outside entity, such as our parents, teachers, siblings, the school system, the news media, or others.

This type of fear is very influential to our decision-making process because it often starts very early in life. Even before you were born, your parents probably worried about you at some level. And then when you came into this world, your parents may have thought they were helping you by warning you of all of the dangers in life, perhaps being overly protective.

Do these sound familiar?

- Some of the warnings were good, such as, "Don't cross the road without looking both ways."
- Or, "Don't run with scissors!"

But some of the warnings could have been completely unfounded. These are good words of wisdom, of course, but there are times when a parent unwittingly overly protects their child. For example, a mother who was mugged some time in her life may not allow her child to go out and play with other children. The child's belief system could be programmed to feel it's a dangerous world out there. And that it's never safe to go outside. Then there are teachers, friends, and other family members who can be an unknowing participant in programming fear into a child. They say words do matter, and this is evidenced by the words that may create unwarranted fears in others.

The news media is especially guilty of programming fear. That's why they call it a "program!" They know if they can keep you in a state of fear, then you are more likely to stay at home, glued to the TV set… Do you need any other evidence to understand why the news is usually negative and depressing?

Caring too Much What Others Think

One of the biggest problems most of us have is this one: caring too much about what other people think.

Most unfounded fears in this area are caused because we care too much. Imagine if you truly didn't care what others thought about you… What would life be like? Think of how free you would feel! For one, since you didn't care what others thought, your fear of public speaking would be completely gone!

Also, you would live a more authentic life…

Ironically, when you don't care what others think, your performance improves too. The professional athlete or singer who cares too much about what fans think won't be able to perform as well as when no one is watching. A solo violinist who cares too much about what others think may blow their performance because of nerves and the fear of playing poorly.

This phenomenon of caring too much goes way back in time. We all have a need to be a part of something—of society, our tribe. And societal ties are strong, because it used to be that if you were rejected by society it could mean death.

So, caring too about what others think is a deeply embedded program within most of us. It's one worth overcoming too!

Lack of Understanding

The lack of understanding is another unfounded fear. We tend to fear what we don't understand. And usually, when we do come to an understanding, we then find there was nothing to fear to begin with. Then the perspective changes and we feel relief. Ah, that wasn't so bad!

Take, for example, a new teenage driver… Not knowing how to drive can cause a teenager to fear the unknown. They may fear the act of driving because they don't have the knowledge yet to drive. But when they study the driving handbook and take driving lessons, the fear subsides as their knowledge grows. The result—more confidence in the act of driving.

For adults and want-to-be-entrepreneurs, a lack of understanding on how to start a business could be a major fear. Yet, once the process is understood, the fear subsides and the inspiration and hard work can begin. That is really rewarding! I can assure you that from personal experiences.

Inaction

The act of not acting escalates and increases fear. When we "feel the fear and do it anyway," we greatly decrease our fear, no matter what it is.

Remember our public speaking scenario? This is a great example for inaction. If we are given the opportunity to speak in public, but turn it down in a spirit of inaction, we are being detrimental to our wellbeing because we give the fear even more power over us. Nothing is worth handing over your control, is it?

Furthermore, this inaction actually breeds more fear. In this example, the fear of public speaking then becomes bigger, and even harder to overcome… It may extend to feeling uncomfortable in groups of people and so on. Stop this dead in its tracks if you have the chance. You're aware now! Take action despite the fear. You will benefit by feeling better about yourself for facing the fear and conquering it. The next time you face it, it'll be easier to overcome. In time, it will simply fade away and be a past memory—a lesson learned long ago.

How to Overcome Fear

The reasons to overcome fear are easy to embrace, but the big question of "how" still lingers, doesn't it? There are several things we can do in order to overcome fear. We've touched on some, in part. Let's dive in further. If you are up for it, think of something you fear and see which one of these ways may just help you move past what is hindering you!

Awareness is Key

People have said awareness and admission of a problem is usually half the battle. Once you are aware you have an unfounded fear, then you can address it. And then you can begin to work on overcoming it...

If it is difficult for you to pinpoint what it is that you fear, then ask yourself, "What do I tend to avoid?" "What do I make excuses for that may actually be hiding a fear?"

When you ask these types of introspective questions, you become more aware of yourself and your fears. This isn't always easy, and at times, it is embarrassing and humbling. However, it is worth it. You've got to know if you're going to do the great things you're capable of.

Most people don't like to admit their fears because they associate it with a sign of weakness. I'd like to counter that it's a sign of strength. It takes a strong person to admit what isn't easy to admit for a great many things—including fear.

Ignoring fear is a temporary fix on a big problem. It leads to excuses, lack of execution, and an overall feeling of discontentment. If you've wondered what's missing, it's likely linked to an unnecessary fear of some sort. Worse yet—it will not remain hidden away forever. When it rears its head—it'll be at the wrong time (which is all the time). This is why awareness is key to your success. When you are aware of the fear, then and only then can you start to do something about it.

MAKING IT HAPPEN!

Challenge Your Fear

*The purpose of challenging your fear is
to check to see if it is real and justified, or not.*

If you have a fear that is real and serves you, then great, keep it. Own it. But if you challenge it and discover it is neither real or serving, then you must do what you can to remove it. Overcome it! This is not really an option.

Start by using logic to challenge your fear. Ask yourself:

- Is what I am afraid of a founded or unfounded fear?
- Is it real?
- How is it stopping me from doing what I want to do in life?

Some questions that you may ask yourself will dig into your past and your childhood. You may find out and realize some fears you have are a result of a childhood decision. Probably not even relevant any longer! You have to find out. Here are some more questions you can ask:

- When did I attain the fear?
- How long have I had it?
- What has it stopped me from doing in my life?
- How has it affected me?

Out of all the questions you've read, the best one is: is it real? There's no better question to use to challenge your fear. Poke it with a stick and see if it is absolutely, undeniably real. Chances are, it's not. Throw the challenge out to yourself then to start changing it. Wipe out the fear and open up your mind to freedom from its grasp.

Get Over the Fear of Failure

Many of us are afraid of failing. And most of us tend to worry about what others will think…

- We worry about what our friends on social media will think;
- We worry about what our family will think;
- We worry about what the neighbors will think;
- We worry about what our friends will think;
- And we worry about what most people think!

But the truth is, failure is the price you pay for success.

Look at some of the world's most successful people—individuals such as Oprah Winfrey, Richard Branson, and Steve Jobs, just to name a few. They all had one thing in common: they aimed so high that even when they failed they landed way above of those who criticized them, and they didn't let what others thought of them affect them. They just kept right on going and didn't let others' opinions sway them. Nor did their failures stop them from attaining their goals and dreams.

Cartoon writer/artist Scott Adams published Dilbert, a strip about an office worker just trying to navigate a day, basically. When asked about his success, he mentioned that he believed failure was a good thing. In his case, when he failed at his sixteen-year-long career in the corporate world, he later used that failure to mock the corporate world through his cartoons.

> *So much of our fear of anything is because of the fear of failure.*
> *But when we see failing from a different angle and a different light,*
> *then the fear can dissipate and lessen.*

Think of all of the inventors of the world who failed over and over before they had success… And businessmen like Walt Disney even. His motto was "Keep moving forward," and he was known to reference how you learn from failure; from success, not so much. Those words are powerful and liberating to anyone with a desire to be innovative with their passions.

You really have to get over this fear of failing thing!

Attain Knowledge

Knowledge is power, but only if we apply the knowledge. And power is fearless. The more you know, the less you have to fear. It is that simple in this case.

- The person that is a constant learner has less to fear than those who don't do anything to advance.
- The entrepreneur/business owner who knows his industry inside-out is not afraid of facing new challenges.
- The professional who knows his profession better than anyone else will always be the best in his subject.

Knowledge about what it is you fear can soften the fear and allow you to overcome it.

Get the Right Advice

When you get the right advice from the right person – a person you trust – regarding the thing that you fear, your fear will naturally begin to wane. Seek out advice from an expert on the very thing that it is that you fear—that will help you to overcome it.

Sometimes, expert advice is priceless. It can stop your fear and allow you to move forward.

Energy Healing Modalities

One of the best ways to overcome fear is to use an energy healing tool. They are not complicated, but they are highly effective. Check out a few of the ideas below. Even look online for success stories with them—because they are abundant.

Emotional Freedom Techniques or Tapping

Emotional Freedom Techniques (EFT) is an energy healing process. It is a form of energy psychology combined with Chinese energy meridian tapping. How it works is somewhat unknown, but the results have been nothing short of astounding.

Its main use is to remove stress, which in turn has very positive effects on the body. But it also can be used to remove any unfounded fear or alleviate guilt from the past and even grant necessary forgiveness to move forward.

People who use EFT have reported getting over their fear of spiders, rats, water, snakes and more. Not only that, but it is easy to learn and easy to do for yourself and others.

Additionally, EFT has been approved by the American Medical Association for patients who suffer from PTSD. Even hospitals like Kaiser Permanent have begun using it for patients.

Self-Hypnosis

Hypnosis is a healing tool that has been effectively used to overcome fear. Although it is not as powerful as EFT, many patients report benefits such as more confidence, better sleep, and the ability to overcome fears.

The benefit to self-hypnosis is that you can listen to it while you sleep and your subconscious mind will still pick up on what was said. Hypnosis can be used for many other types of problems too, including addictive behaviors with food, drugs, alcohol, smoking cessation, and self-esteem.

Meditation

Meditation can be used to calm the mind and body down, to get centered, and to assist the mind and body in fully relaxing. This is another excellent tool you can use to overcome fear. However, meditation is more for overall health. Regardless, you can use every day in order to overcome fear. You could do a guided meditation to show you what a moment could be like without fear to start training your subconscious mind to let go of the old, and welcome in the new, more fearless you.

Reiki

Reiki is another energy healing tool more closely related to EFT than anything else. The practitioner uses their own energy with their hands held about a foot away from the client. No touching is involved and many people claim to have excellent results with it. You can even get Reiki massages, which bring relaxation and a new awareness to your mind about your body and the energy that is always in motion within it.

**There are other forms of energy healing modalities out there and you can explore them to find out which one works best for you.

A Fearless Day

In summary, fear can be either beneficial or a hindrance. Some fears, such as the fear of dangerous wild animals are appropriate, even useful. But the days of us having to worry about being eaten by powerful predators are pretty much over for most of us.

It's really the unfounded fears that cause us so much grief. They usually begin in childhood. Parents, teachers, and other influential adults usually program them into us, not out of malice, but out of caring. But the result is the same.

Fear is one of the biggest obstacles that humans face in our lives. Isn't it strange to think that a fear you may have made up has stopped you from doing so much? It happens all the time, and they are often products of our own imaginations. Like a computer program, we downloaded them from the people in our environments.

Ultimately, regardless of where fear comes from, it should be challenged and overcome. You owe it to yourself, if nothing else.

When you overcome fear, you conquer life. It's really that simple.

2 | Self-Improvement

**Excellence is not a destination.
It is a continuous journey that never ends.**

One of the secrets of great leadership is the desire to focus on self-improvement. Before you can begin to influence or inspire others, you need to:

1. Work on yourself from the inside out;
2. And do so consistently.

We are always a work-in-progress. The quest for excellence is never meant to be a destination; it's a never-ending odyssey of discovering, rediscovering, understanding, and developing yourself.

Throughout your journey, you are guaranteed to face a variety of circumstances in life. This includes your career, business, and personal life. There will be new environments, new business associates, new opportunities, and new roles for work. When it comes to your personal life, there may be marriages, starting a family, divorce, or losing a loved one. These are serious matters. How do you cope with the pressures and stress that come with life's constant changes?

Your ability to handle life's challenges depends on how well you keep pace with shifting times. The only way to do this effectively is through self-improvement.

No matter what situation you are in, there is always room to learn, grow, and improve. Whether you are aspiring, at the peak of your career, or one who already has a lot of accomplishments behind you, you should never cease to seek the best possible version of your present self. This is how you evolve, and there is no better way to attain unshakeable self-confidence and find genuine happiness than embarking on the continuous journey of self-development.

Self-Knowledge is the Beginning of Self-Improvement

"If you know the enemy and know yourself, you need not fear the outcome of a hundred battles. If you know yourself but not the enemy, for every victory gained you will also suffer a defeat. If you know neither the enemy nor yourself, you will succumb in every battle."
— **Sun Tzu, The Art of War**

The first and most important step in improving yourself is an honest evaluation of your own personality. To know the enemy is to know your weakness—your dark side, if you will. Paraphrased for practical applications other than war, the quote above would read: "If you want to succeed, you have to know your strengths and weaknesses. If you only know your strengths and not your weaknesses, for every success, there is a corresponding measure of failure. If you do not know you strengths or weaknesses, you are bound to fail in every turn." How does the thought of that make you feel? Do you want to succeed or fail at every turn?

You want success, of course!

When I first arrived in the United States, I spoke no English. I was fifteen and I started working in the farms, picking strawberries, tomatoes, and tobacco in the fields of Florida, Georgia, and Kentucky under the scorching hot sun every day. I also worked in restaurants as a dishwasher and was a factory worker. I wasn't making enough money, but I was making a lot more than what I could have made in my country. This is when I realized that even low paying jobs in America were way better than other parts of the world. That's when I saw a big opportunity—the only way for me to advance was to learn to speak basic English, at minimal.

But how did I do this?

I found a church that provided free basic English classes twice a week. I attended all the free evening classes for the next twelve months and finally could speak some English. I thought I was on top of my game. Then when I started to work for Mr. Shapiro, he noticed my English was not at a level where I could communicate with his staff, so he offered to pay for me to take more classes. This kind gesture helped shape more of my vocabulary and my confidence was established. From then on, I made the decision to never stop learning.

Eventually, when I had developed my skills, I learned a trade in the construction industry and I started my own company. This entire experience still reminds me how important it is to have continuous self-improvement in life. To this day, I continuously read books, attend workshops, seminars to keep learning new things. This also helps me remain relevant and grow my network.

> *The secret of very successful people is that they know themselves very well. They leverage on their strengths and they improve on their weaknesses.*

Genuine and lasting self-improvement can only be attained from the process of gaining true self-knowledge.

8 Ways to Improve Your Self-Awareness

Through these 8 ways to learn the art of becoming more self-aware, you will be able to give yourself the necessary tools you need to start pursuing this worthy – and necessary – reflection of your life in any given moment.

MAKING IT HAPPEN!

1. Know your strengths and weaknesses

Do you find yourself feeling superior or inferior toward other people based on their (or your) strengths and weaknesses? There is no reason to be proud of your strengths. In truth, you are only as good as your strongest weakness.

Alternatively, there is no reason to be ashamed of your weaknesses, because your weaknesses have the potential to help you grow in the most incredible ways. They can become one of your greatest strengths.

Like yin and yang, your life is interplay of both strengths and weaknesses; one cannot exist independently of the other.

This is not common knowledge, but it is truth. There is a coinciding weakness for any strength and vice versa. Indecisiveness may be a weakness, but can be balanced by patience. You may sound negative, but you are just being realistic. In the same manner, you may create an impression of being arrogant when you really just ooze with self-confidence.

On the other hand, humility may be a virtue, but timidity can take you nowhere. You may appear very calm – and it may be impressive – but in truth, you're just being emotionless. You may be a very responsible person but that strong sense of responsibility can also make you boring. Do you get the idea? If you embark on the journey of soul searching, you will discover these yin yangs within you. If you know your weaknesses, you can avoid engaging in activities where you are not very effective. Example, you may be stubborn, but it's because you are very dedicated. Your stubbornness may not make you a great salesman, but your dedication could make you a very good lawyer. You must take time to develop your strengths and manage your weaknesses. This is how you prepare yourself to navigate life's twists and turns.

There are two ways to manage your weaknesses:

1. Strive to make yourself better;
2. Or, just accept it and let others who are better at it do it for you.

The key is identifying which weaknesses are ones you can live with, and which could wreck you if left unaddressed. Intelligent persons tend to be messy and disorganized because their focus lies on what they consider more important. Should you shift your focus on housekeeping instead of trying to change the world? Would that help you become the change you want to see? I'm not suggesting that. There are things that you can easily pay for – a secretary or a housekeeper – but not everyone can do your job. You don't have to be a rocket scientist to understand the logic of this.

But what if your weakness is a character flaw that just keeps turning your clients off or making your people quit? This big question needs evaluation. The conclusion should be that you want to lessen that weakness, at minimal. To do otherwise is costly. Sure, some people can afford to hire reputation managers or personnel managers, but no one can avoid interpersonal interaction all the time. This is when improving your attitude toward others is a must. The same thing is true with your spending habits. If your spending habits are the obstacles in attaining your millionaire goals, you really have to rein yourself in.

It may sound cliché, but life does require balance. You must strive to find it and then be intuitive enough to maintain it.

In the end, you must remember that the greater your strength, the bigger the corresponding weakness probably is. Learn to maximize your potential through self-awareness about who you are and who you want to be.

2. Know your temperament

There is a proto-psychological theory known as the "four temperaments." Most people fall into one of these categories.

- **Choleric**
Are you firm, forceful, practical, straightforward, ambitious, analytical, enthusiastic, goal-oriented, driven, and confrontational? These are the traits of a choleric person. Cholerics have a natural talent to motivate

and influence others. Always ready to lead, they want to take charge of everything. Advocates of tough love, they tend to help people by challenging them. If you are a choleric, you will succeed if you choose to be an entrepreneur, manager, CEO, influencer, preacher, or are in any role that requires leadership, motivation, and productivity. Cholerics are dominant, seemingly arrogant, contentious, and condescending.

*If you feel you are a Choleric,
you understand what quality to play up and what to improve on.*

- **Sanguine**

Are you bubbly, chatty, transparent, boisterous, energetic, cheerful, optimistic, buoyant, and carefree? These are just a few of the traits of a Sanguine. Creative and artistic, they are often the life of the party—with them, there is no dull moment. But fun as they are to be around, they aren't particularly trustworthy and reliable. They talk more than listen and they shun dull and boring people. The best career choice for Sanguines are celebrities, fashion designers, make-up artists, comedians, sales and marketing reps, masters of ceremonies, auctioneers, and charismatic politicians. They also make great hospital workers because of their ability to cheer patients.

If you are a Sanguine, this will help you identify your weaknesses and manage them so you can soar like an eagle.

- **Phlegmatic**

Reliable, supportive, levelheaded, committed, patient, gentle, and kind are some of the qualities of a Phlegmatic. Submissive introverts, they would rather please others than resist to avoid conflict at all costs. They tend to own mistakes in order to avoid trouble. Devoid of ambition, they are content to be at peace with others. They are super sensitive to the feelings of others and careful not to hurt. Extremely loyal and trustworthy, they are ideal parents and spouses. The best career paths for Phlegmatics are as nurses, teachers, psychologists, counselors, social workers, administrators, engineers, supervisors, managers, and foremen.

If you are a Phlegmatic, your friends and family are the luckiest of persons, but you need to cultivate your assertiveness to survive and excel in this dog-eat-dog society.

- **Melancholic**

   If you are an idealist, perfectionist, over analytical, pessimistic, tenacious, stubborn, organized, introverted, sensitive, calm, quiet, tactful, cautious, and task oriented, then you are Melancholic. You never act without a plan and never make rash decisions. You cannot tolerate wrong so you can be very contentious, yet you back your arguments with logical explanations and pleading. You always seek perfection in everything, so even your best can't be good enough at times. You have high ideals and are easily distressed when things don't go your way so you are often broken hearted, thus melancholic. The perfect career choices for Melancholics are painters, writers, musicians, poets. Artists are capable of delivering masterpieces if their hearts are broken. Just remember, as you progress, the key is not to demand perfection.

   If you are Melancholic, understanding your personality will greatly improve your self-awareness and help you identify your strengths and weaknesses.

3. Examine your personal values

Your core beliefs define your character, the very principles that you are willing to fight and even die for. What are the set of principles that you adhere to and how well founded are they? Do you honor them consistently? Or do you hold a double standard morality?

Did you know that there are over 400 personal values that you can find online? I encourage you to take time to seek these out and review them. Write down the top ten values that resonate with you most. Remember, there are no wrong or right choices or priorities. It's your life, so it's your choice. Some of the most desirable values are:

Love	Fidelity
Faith	Responsibility
Altruism	Generosity

Boldness	Discipline
Freedom	Dignity
Honesty	Health
Honor	Wealth
Humility	Trustworthiness
Integrity	Sincerity
Justice	Gratitude
Kindness	Hope

It's easy to idealize and choose the values that appear better than others, but you cannot determine personal core values this way. To hone in on your real values, try reliving your best moments and the values that you honored during those times. Then try to recall you worst moments, those times when you were angry, discouraged, sad, or did something shameful. What were the values you suppressed? These tips can help identify your values, which you really should be able to know without much effort at all.

Once you've identified your core values, ask yourself: are they aligned with your thoughts, words, and deeds? Can your friends see the same values that you think you have? Your success depends largely on how clear you are about why you do what you do.

4. Identify your interests and passions

"Choose a job you love and you will never have to work a day in your life." This quote from Confucius explains why people who build a career around their deep interests are the happiest creations in the universe. What are the things you love thinking and doing most? Include your passions and hobbies! You may have relegated some of them in the attic of your memories because real life pressures suppressed them. If you are passionate about the arts, yet decided upon an engineering career, chances are you will be less successful than your peers whose interests are in numbers. Think what it would be like to be able to make a living out of the things you love doing the best.

5. Know your biorhythms

Most people function best during the day, but others function best at night (the night owl), when there is less noise and commotion. Are you a night person or a morning person? What time of day do you give your peak performance? Night people are rarely at their best in the morning. Likewise, morning people seldom have their best energy in the evening. This is important to understand about yourself, particularly as you pursue greater potential. If you have been forcing yourself to work during the day when you are a night person, your productivity is greatly compromised. When you work in accordance to your innate biology, you have more chances of succeeding than forcing yourself to work in a schedule that doesn't work well for you. If you are in sync with your biology and you find a mate and business partners who have the same biorhythms as you do, you save a lot of time and energy and achieve optimum performance.

6. Find the purpose and meaning for your existence

Everyone is born with a mission, but not everyone has found or fulfilled their purpose in life. You may be trapped in a job you hate while you see people around you shining brightly, connected and fulfilled by their career of choice. Taking note of this can cause envy and anger, but stop feeling this way as quickly as possible! Use it for inspiration to find your purpose in life.

Your purpose is a journey and the right path that leads to it is by following your passions. You are gifted with life, so discover it, live it, and live it passionately and purposefully. Take the case of Mother Teresa, she was a Roman Catholic nun who devoted her life to serving the poor and destitute around the world. She spent many years in Calcutta, India, where she founded the Missionaries of Charity, a religious congregation devoted to helping those in great need. In 1979, Mother Teresa was awarded the Nobel Peace Prize and became a symbol of charitable, selfless work.

"It is not how much we do, but how much love we put in the doing. It is not how much we give, but how much love we put in the giving."
— **Mother Teresa**

7. Observe your mind

"It all begins and ends in the mind. What you give power to, has power over you."
— **Leon Brown**

Every day your mind is conditioned by the media, by events, and by people around you. Sometimes you forget to think for yourself and hand over too much power to the news, shows, or media bombardment. The troubling messages these mediums deliver linger in your mind and influence your emotions. It's time to reclaim your power to control what you allow to invade and dominate your thoughts. Observing your mind can help you separate your thoughts from awareness. You see, your awareness observes your thoughts. Because of this, the more you practice mindfulness (the awareness), the more you realize your thoughts are not you, and that you have the power to control them, instead of them controlling you. This is a form of meditation that you can do around the clock, even in the hectic, jam-packed world you live in.

8. Indulge yourself!

What are the things that you've always wanted to do yet kept pushing off due to economic reasons or time constraints? Think of what makes you happy and do those things! If not now, when? And why not now? It could be a trip to the Bahamas or to the Holy Land. Don't hold yourself back. By all means, fall in love under the Spanish sun. Wet your feet and trousers at the edge of the ocean. Swim naked under the silver moonlight. Share a kiss on the white sand with a summer fling or your true love. Take a nap in a hammock. Watch fireflies on hot nights. Build elaborate sandcastles. Connect with nature. Just do!

Savor quiet evenings with your loved one, reminiscing precious memories as you lounge about the fire. Sample the range of broiled seafood in varied eating spots alongside the beach. Brave the karaoke bars. Read your favorite book. Treat yourself to a spa. Buy that expensive outfit. Whatever you decide to do, just let go! Pamper your body and your soul, and you will feel good about yourself. If you are kind to yourself, more doors will be opened to self-knowledge. If you are friends with yourself, you can take an honest look at your true self, not only superficially – as in a mirror – but inwardly, without pretensions and charade.

Expect Improvement

These are the major improvements that come as a consequence of self-awareness:

- **Inner harmony**
  If there is no conflict in your feelings, reason, and values, you tend to make wise, rational, and confident decisions—even in the face of difficulties. If you have inner harmony, success comes easily and naturally, but if you haven't "arrived" yet, you are not disheartened by that.

- **Self-control**
  Buddha is quoted as saying, "A man who conquers himself is greater than one who conquers a thousand men in battle." The hardest battle you may face is against yourself. Once you have conquered yourself, you will become unstoppable, because if you have conquered your toughest opponent, what obstacle can possibly withstand you?

- **Tenacity**

  If you know what you really want, you will abide by your own set of values and principles. There will be no easy succumbing to peer or social pressure. Because you are sure of yourself, you will persist through all kinds of challenges and will never give up.

- **Compassion**

  If you are honest enough to admit your faults and shortcomings, you will have no problem empathizing with and tolerating others. A self-righteous person is always ready to point an accusing finger to those who err, oblivious of their struggles and difficulties.

- **Authenticity**

  Knowing and being who you truly are gives you a profound sense of freedom to experience life in a richer and more exciting way.

- **Receptivity**

  Inability to handle criticism is a very common weakness of people who are in denial. Self-awareness helps you be open to criticism and facts or perspectives that challenge yours. Being open to criticism is a form of self-discovery—looking at yourself through the eyes of others. If you can be that honest with yourself, you can easily identify the faults and desires you want to eradicate. This leads to fewer vices and issues obstructing your growth. Once you have addressed your faults, weaknesses, temptations, fears, and the other things that hinder growth, there's no stopping you. If you can master your thoughts and overcome yourself, you will be able to make life better, healthier, wealthier, and happier for you. Guess who else benefits from that? Those around you!

Arm Yourself with Self-Knowledge

Self-awareness allows you to assess how your feelings and perceptions affect your thinking and actions. Your actions are results of what and how you think and the reason why you do what you do. Once you become a master of your thoughts, you also become the master of your behavior. As you begin to discover yourself, your path toward personal development and growth widens. Gradually, you will find huge improvements in your relationships, career, business, health, wealth, and overall happiness.

So arm yourself daily with questions about yourself—your thoughts, reactions, behavior, preferences, values, interests, purpose, and visions. Answers give you certainty, which gives you security. The problem is security sometimes robs you of the opportunity to grow. New questions give you doubt the doubt you need. Why? Because doubt creates discomfort. Discomfort makes you seek for answers. And the seeking for answers makes you grow. Become a curious child who doesn't stop asking for information because they have an insatiable appetite for knowledge. Just turn the game on you—and you should be able to eventually answer the toughest questions on one of the toughest subjects, which is you.

"It's not as much about who you used to be as it is about who you choose to be."
— Sanhita Baruah

MAKING IT HAPPEN!

3 | Time Management

Time…it's one of your most intimate relationships. As with any relationship, it has its ups and downs. To make it through those times, stability and trust are necessary. They are what bring forth the peace and pleasure. Therefore, a time management strategy is crucial to managing and maintaining balance and confidence in your life.

Where this gets tricky is in understanding how time is also a versatile word—with no definition that is suitable for all, so it is important for you to define the term for yourself. Your systems for organizing, your goals, and you priorities vary according to your personal preferences. Hence, your strengths and weaknesses, commitments and lifestyle, and responsibilities all contribute to the formation of a time management strategy.

As you read my strategies for managing time, reflect upon your own interpretation of the word and your ongoing relationship with it. This is important, because you must tailor your management plan to your individual needs.

External Time

External time is the measurement that everyone follows because we are all aware of it. It allows us to coordinate activities with others because it is structured and constant.

We measure external time by seconds, minutes, hours, weeks, months, days, and years. We base this type of time on the rotation and orbit of the earth and it is the standard for which we all live our lives. It is a physical reality; therefore, it is beyond our control. Our only hope for harmony with external time is to adjust our way of life to accommodate it.

Additionally, we are constantly aware of external time because we have scheduled events, appointments, meetings, and deadlines to keep. Our punctuality, according to external time, affects both our personal and professional relationships. If we disregard the clock, we could lose our jobs, damage our personal partnerships, and miss opportunities.

It's easy to agree we need this time. However, watching the clock is not always healthy, and we should not allow external time to govern our every action. External time sets limits on our creativity, productivity, and overall well-being. Because this time is rigid and constant, we feel pressure to produce all we can, so we do not allow even a fraction of time to get away from us. This creates stress and anxiety, tension and worry, and frustration. External time decides whether we succeed or fail.

External time consists of three identities, the:

- Past
- Present
- Future

The past is gone forever, the present is THIS moment and the only thing we can really mold, and the future is nothing more than an ideal, which keeps us striving.

Thoughts of the future often consume us because it is always coming after us, and we can do nothing to slow it down or speed up its movement. While it is best for our health to stay in the present, our thoughts and feelings are often divided between the things we failed to do in the past and the things we need to achieve in the future. This constant battle between these two phases of external time, and our present being, disrupts our natural flow. We cannot reach the highest level of productivity if the past and future consume us.

With the future, we see possibility. When we are incapable of enjoying our present time, we begin to think of the future, or reminisce about the past because we hope for better things to come or we want to relive better times. In other words, we escape the present to avoid ill emotions or impending disappointment. While we are ALWAYS physically rooted in the present, seldom do we find ourselves there mentally, which opens up avenues to poor time management.

Since external time is unavoidable and something that we cannot disregard, we must live within its boundaries and we must follow its rules. It is also paramount that we consider how our lives would play out in a state of chaos without time, which is why we should begin to look at external time in a positive way and learn to adapt our life to complement it.

Internal Time

Internal time is NOT concrete. In fact, we can best describe it as a SENSE of time because it is not measurable.

The minutes on a clock or the days on a calendar never comprise internal time, and its structure varies for every person, altering with each activity. Since internal time is an abstract concept, there is no clear-cut definition of it. It lies somewhere within your feelings, thoughts, and eventual actions; therefore, every individual has some semblance of control over this type of time, even if it is ever-adjusting due to new circumstances.

Have you ever found yourself engrossed in a project, and you simply lost track of time? Did you ever experience a sense of timelessness? This is YOUR internal time. Within this realm, you do not feel the limitations or pressures external time sets. This freedom allows you to accomplish undertakings that might seem impossible at their start. Certainly, you have been in the midst of moments where you were positive that you would miss a deadline, but through some miracle, you did not. Your feeling of desperation coupled with a sense of urgency granted you an endless amount of internal time, as you let go of external time because it did not suit your needs.

> *Since we often limit ourselves by following the strict measures external time, we have often ignored the precious value of internal time.*

However, it is in the realm of internal time that you become the most creative and productive because nothing matters except what you are working to accomplish. It's a beautiful and rewarding moment. You become so absorbed in your mission that external time is no longer relevant, and its absence is bliss.

Unfortunately, we cannot live on internal time alone, as lovely as it does sound. In our world, it just is not possible because we coordinate our lives with those of others based on external time. So how do you channel internal time with all those factors working against it? The key is "involvement." Engagement leads to total engrossment, which brings us to a sense of timelessness. Have you ever noticed how your degree of involvement in a task directly correlates to the quality of the final product and the efficiency of its completion? The more you are heavily involved in a project, the more likely you are to do a great job at it.

Tapping into your internal time produces a myriad of benefits.

- You reach the highest level of creativity and productivity, while lowering stress levels.
- The timelessness of internal time frees you from the pressures and the oppressive nature that comes with the bond of external time.
- Through internal time, your overall quality of work will improve, your relationships will strengthen, and, in essence, you will find greater peace in your life.

So, how should you create a time management system that works for you and keeps you on track in a healthy way? It goes back to that ever-important word: balance.

Individual Perception of Time

> *Even though external time is constant and we cannot change it, our individual perception of time varies greatly from person to person.*

Before you can hone your time management skills, you first have to take a moment for self-reflection and answer the following questions:

- What time constraints did you experience while growing up?
- How do you handle situations when you are running late?
- Do you often feel that time works against you?
- What was your immediate family's attitude toward time?
- Do you feel lost when you are unaware of the time?
- Do you make time for leisure activities?
- How well do you handle leisure time?
- Do you allow time to control you?
- How do you define the phrase "on time?"
- Do you feel like managing your time is always a desperate act?

By answering these questions in a truthful way, you will discover the underlying influences shaping your time awareness. For example, if you grew up in a very organized household with a time-efficient atmosphere, your attitude regarding time is presumably significantly different from the person who was immersed in unorganized chaos. Your transition into effective time management becomes smoother when you determine why you feel you need more control of time and better strategies for managing it.

Has time become your enemy? If you feel time works against you and no matter how hard you try to get it under control, it always defeats, you have an unhealthy relationship with it. Time is not the executioner, and this mentality is a self-defeating notion. Time is simply a "thing" that is neither your enemy nor ally, so it is important to accept it, and never use it as a scapegoat.

I believe it helps to acknowledge how time does not bend to your will. You might believe that it controls you and you have no power in its grasp, but time does not have a conscience, so it is not working against you to create misery in your life. It does nothing but provide the world with a sense of pace, and it is disinterested in how you feel about its stride.

Knowing all this, you can take the step to get time under better control in your life. Your initial step to becoming time-efficient begins with an attitude adjustment. Take blame for your ineffectual time management and then take control of time through sound strategies that fall in line with your perception of it.

Work and Leisure Time

Some people value their leisure time, and yet they abuse it. Quite often, these people will have a good grip on their time management while they are working, but when it comes to leisure, they have no idea what to do with themselves and the time they allotted for it. Time and the management of it is not a constant for them; instead, it changes from a comfortable ally to an enemy that has invaded their perfect world. Time for leisure can cause an organized work professional to panic.

Is this you?

If it is, relax and consider this: it is not time creating the tension, instead, it is a lack of VALUE recognition. For those of you who fear leisure time, you might simply be afraid of wasting the time you set aside to play. Ultimately, you will do one of two things.

1. You will overflow your days and nights with endless work activities.
2. You set aside time for leisure, but do nothing productive with it. Because you believe you have no real control over your leisure time, you do not make any effort to use it wisely, therefore it feels like a time waster.

There is a quick fix to this dilemma. Apply the same principles of time you use at work to your leisure time. Realize "time" remains the same regardless of whether you are at work or not. If you manage your time well while working, you already have a value system and a time management strategy that is functional. Since you already know how to prioritize, set goals, and find a balance between the urgent and trivial at work, simply apply the same standards to your leisure time.

If that person I just described doesn't sound like you, perhaps what I share next is more in line with who you are.

Do you value your leisure time and fear your time at work? Maybe you are unhappy with your job or feel as though some agent in the world is forcing "work" upon you. Subconsciously or blatantly, you create a resistance to your professional life and put all your effort into a well-coordinated strategy for managing your leisure time. Because leisure activity is the only enjoyable part of your day, you spend it in a fulfilling manner as your work life crumbles in chaos. You accomplish very little at work because you put no effort into a time management strategy, because you feel like it is not worth the effort.

This mentality creates a vicious cycle.

Inside of this confused existence, time passes quickly for you when you spend it doing leisure activities, but it stands still while you are at work. You must adjust your attitude. You can still enjoy your leisure more than the time you spend at work, but for your health and well-being, it is imperative for you to analyze what empowers you to make the most of your leisure time and apply those measures to your time at work.

For example, if you have created clearly defined goals in your leisure time, use them at work as well. While your values and goals might be different within the two realms, you still have a good foundation to build upon just by incorporating the basics. Then, as your time management skills strengthen at work, you will find you get just as much fulfillment at the office as you do from your leisure time, although it will be a very different kind of satisfaction.

If all this fails, consider this: many of the joys of leisure time are dependent on some of the returns that work offers.

Punctuality

Some people make it a habit of delaying everything they are going to do eventually. It could be arriving late, whether it is a social function, work, or personal appointment. They just have no sense of time's importance—or at least it seems that way. These people have developed a reputation for being late or not delivering. They seldom like the reputation, but it does provide an excuse everyone in their life has come to accept. However, being chronically late does eventually backfire.

While it may be expected or accepted, chronic tardiness shows a lack of respect for other people. Furthermore, you might miss opportunities to take on responsibilities at work or in your personal life because others feel as if they cannot rely on you, and it is probably true.

For those of you who are perpetually late, there are a few things that you can do to curb your habit:

- You can trick yourself by setting your clocks forward or you can just plan to be at your destination 15 minutes before others expect you to be there. Therefore, if you are normally 15 minutes behind schedule, this tactic will get you there on time.
- You can schedule 10 minutes of downtime between activities, so you give yourself some slack from event to event.

These two strategies are helpful, but what you truly need is to develop an effective time management system and find the determination to follow. This will carry you further than mind tricks to get on track will (in the long term).

In addition, some people simply have no regard for time. Let's be blunt—this is not good.

You or someone you know may think this is an idealistic way to live life, but this creates as many problems as believing time is the enemy. If you disregard time, you have no real guidelines for accomplishing things and "goal" becomes a foreign word because deadlines do not exist. Essentially, you have separated yourself from the motivators of the world, and while you might believe you are completely FREE as a result, you are fooling yourself. Your lifestyle still indicates that you are just as time-obsessed as all other people, and the obsession owns you.

If you are resistant to the idea of external and internal time, you give it endless play.

You don't need to obsess about time and its constraints, but try to recognize that it will forever influence your life and that you must control it, so that it never controls you.

Passing Time

Have you ever felt like life abandoned you on the "time" highway? Every day people pass you by because they have their lives in order and manage their time in a productive way, but you…you stand still.

How about feeling overwhelmed? Do the restraints of the hours in each day burden you? Most everyone feels that way, at least occasionally. When putting together a time management strategy, it is important to determine why you feel like you never have the time you need.

> *Ask yourself this question: if I were given more time, how would I use it?*

Pretend you have an extra ten hours tomorrow and write down what you would do with the additional time. Then, go through the list and rank each activity according to its importance to you. Finally, look at the first few items on the list that you designated as the most important. Have these activities been pushed aside for a while now? Do you feel the items are important enough to deal with right away, even though they are important to you? Are these activities the reasons why you need more time in the day? Are you strategizing ways to manage your time better?

Begin to look at your life objectively, and examine the reoccurring factors that keep you from getting ahead. Like most people, several minor details in your life add up to one or two big problems. You may or may not even realize what the setbacks are. Be curious about your real relationship with time. Ask the following questions:

- Do you attempt to fit two days of work into a single day more than once a week?
- Do you have difficulty saying no to a request for your time?
- Do you have realistic goals and aspirations?

MAKING IT HAPPEN!

- Do you procrastinate often?
- Do you daydream often?
- Do you find your work to be pleasurable?
- Do you fill your day with matters you must attend to right away?
- Are you a perfectionist?
- Do you swim in a sea of sticky notes?
- Do you rush around constantly, while everyone else enjoys his or her work and leisure time?
- Are you often working on two things at once?
- Do you lose things often?
- Do you enjoy starting new projects, but rarely complete them?

Chances are, you answered "yes" to at least one of the questions, and maybe even several of them. Consider the reasons behind the "yes" answers, and take a moment to analyze why you daydream, lose things, or have sticky-note reminders at every stop. Your reasons for the actions should be your concern. No need to dig deep, basic reasons will do. You cannot defeat a problem without first getting to the heart of it.

If you answered "no" to every question, do not assume you are in the clear. First, if you are concerned about your time management skills, problem exists somewhere. It might be necessary for you to dig deeper into your daily schedule and comb through all of the details before you to discover what is tripping you up. Perhaps you have formed habits you do not even consider because they have become such a part of your being—like checking email every 10 minutes, for example. Therefore, look at those important activities you never find the time to do, and consider why you have chosen to push aside those particular, important items. What stands in the way of you accomplishing things important to you? Try to be as specific as possible as you rattle the cage of your mind.

Additionally, understand that I did not design the exercise to assist you in placing blame on yourself or anyone else. Rather, its intention is to help you find reason behind your hectic life. Once you discover the areas needing immediate attention, you can work efficiently on strategies to improve your time management.

> *Do not be upset if it seems like your life needs work because we can all improve the mechanics of our lives in one way or another.*

Finally, again, remember "time" is not the guilty party here; your use of time is the culprit. You must take control of every day, and adapt your life to complement the external time life gives you. Depending on your degree of desire and desperation, you might only need a couple of hours, or you might need couple of months to fix your time management concerns. Regardless of the amount of time it costs you to find the perfect strategy for your life, developing good time management skills will assist you in getting to a place where time is finally at your command.

Track Your Use of Time

We have established that time is constant; it cannot be changed to fit your needs or anyone else's needs. We all have a certain amount of time allotted to us, but how we choose to use our time varies widely. To be successful in time management, you must first look at how you presently use your time.

Follow these steps to start tracking!

1. Keep a record of all of your activities during a 24-hour timeframe. Yes, this will take "time" from your day, and you may even feel the necessity to record the time you spend recording your day. However, this is an easy way to get a look at your habits and how many of them are a waste of your time.

2. Create three columns on a piece of paper. Title the first column "Beginning Time." In this column, you will record the hour and the minute in which you begin an activity. The second column will be "Activity." The "activity" column will include with details of the task you performed. For instance, instead of simply writing "work" you would write: "schedule to meet with customer to discuss project." And instead of "exercise," you put: "jogged three miles at the gym." Furthermore,

make a note of all distractions, interruptions, breaks, and commute times. The third column will be "Ending Time." Here, you record the exact time you ended the activity.

3. After 24 hours, calculate the amount of time that was productive and the amount of time that was a waste. You might be surprised to find out you accomplish more in a day than you thought you did, or you may find you waste more time than you make use of. Regardless, now you have an idea where all of your time is going, and you can start planning a strategy.

Do not throw your log away. Hold on to your findings, and in a few weeks, repeat the exercise and a look at how the two logs compare. By then, you should be showing some progress, and if you are not, you will want to re-evaluate the strategy you are using. Or be honest with yourself and admit you haven't really given the proper efforts.

The Realities of LIFE and Time Management

We must face it; our desire for skilled time management does not always result in a happy ending. We live in the REAL WORLD, and the reality of the REAL WORLD has a way of rearranging our most carefully crafted plans. Therefore, we must prepare for every outcome that we can imagine, while understanding we will miss a few.

Life is one unrestrained curve ball, but as long as we accept the possibility of setbacks, we are actually further ahead than we might think.

As you begin to analyze your use of time and make a plan for how you can make the most of it, pencil in TIME for interruptions. By allowing for surprises, whether it is an emergency, meltdown, or a lapse in memory, your daily plan will go unaffected, and you will not feel like you failed when you get off schedule.

If you pretend you are superhuman and put together a strategy to get things done in less time, it is possible—and it is also a potential disaster! You could end up doing a poor job at the tasks in front of you, or your plan could back up, could lead to further delays and crush your confidence. Preparing a realistic timeframe for the completion of tasks is essential for good time management.

Many unanticipated things come our way on a daily basis and life is full of little surprises, some good and some not. Do not allow them to get you down. Your plan for time management is just that, A PLAN; it is not a law that you must abide by without fail or you punish yourself. No, your strategic time management plan should never become ruling force in your life. The PLAN is a guideline you create to HELP you accomplish what is important to you without losing your life's meaning as you search for time tranquility.

Prioritize Your Time

So far, you should have done the following to construct your time management plan:

- Worked through the psychological factors involved in your current time management issues
- Made a log of your daily activities so that know where you spend your time, both productively and wastefully
- Figured out the life activities that are of the most important to you

With this knowledge at hand, the next step is to take action, and that begins with learning to prioritize your time. Ask yourself these questions:

- What do you NEED from your daily life?
- What do you WANT from your daily life?
- Where do you WANT TO GO in your daily life?
- Where do you want to BE at the end of EACH DAY?

These types of questions help you understand what is most important to you. The focus of solid time management is figuring out how to spend every moment in an appropriate and effective manner. Unless you make a list of priorities, you cannot assess your progress from day to day to see if your strategy is working well. Therefore, take the time to get it right.

Break down the priorities into four different priorities, which are:

- Home
- Family
- Work
- Personal

Within these priorities, brainstorm what is important to you. It does not matter if your list is long or short; honestly and truth is what is important.

Once you have compiled a list, circle the top ten items that have the most significance to you. Then, rank the ten priorities in order of least-to-most important. In this moment, be selfish. Do not think of anyone's priorities other than your own or this will not work.

Once your list is created, hold it on your person, wherever you go, and refer to it often. This is really effective because when you have those moments where you question how you spend your time, you will have a guide that points you in the right direction. Do not hesitate to make changes to your list either, because as you grow and life evolves, you should expect change.

Important Priorities

"Important" and "urgent" are two words that are straightforward. When it comes to time management, they are necessary parts of the solution. "Important" priorities have value and significance, while "urgent" priorities call for immediate attention, but are not necessarily important. In order to prioritize properly, you need understand the difference between the two.

> *People with poor time management skills consider almost every task an urgent priority, which makes it impossible to make decisions when everything demands attention right away.*

Furthermore, the decision-making process wastes an abundance of time, which delays those "urgencies" even longer. Your phone is ringing, your emails are screaming at you, you are late for work, your child is hungry, and you have not planned the weekend trip. So, what do you make a priority? While it is hard to ignore the technology that needs your attention, should it become your priority?

Our lives should never become reactionary. Conscious thought should guide your decisions, and when it does not, you push important matters to chase urgent ones. The important things are the ones that have the most influence on our daily lives, and they should demand our attention. I do not want to dictate what you should put first in your life, but I assume your values come first, and you find those values in your family, your personal health, and your overall security. Those things become what is important and need to be prioritized when planning your activities.

An abundance of urgencies will keep you constantly on the defensive, which means you will never be on "the offensive."

Furthermore, consider that your "urgent" matters go to the critical stage because they were not resolved in a timely manner. Break the vicious cycle or chaos will always pursue you. You can create categories and make adjustments that help you take care of what you need to, saving on your sanity, while also giving you a sense of accomplishment. Try this:

- First, categorize the activities in your life that are the important and urgent. These items should take precedence over everything else.

- The second category consists of activities that are important but NOT urgent.

- The third category includes the activities that are urgent but NOT important.

- The final category consists of the NOT urgent and NOT important items. These activities are "fun," but have nothing to do with your values.

For me, I always start my day by hitting the gym to workout. During my workouts I listen to audiobooks, podcasts, or anything to help boost my energy. I believe a healthy life leads to a happy life. As a result of being healthier, I will have more focus for everything I do in a day.

After my workout, I call and talked to my wife about family matters, I do a few hours of work. I communicate with key employees, new and existing clients, secure more deals, and so on. And from there I plan and adjust my schedule accordingly for the next days.

Lastly, I will run other errands and then head back home to do things I like and spend time with my family. Before bed, I take time to read a book.

To help you categorize your priorities and important activities, use the following examples:

- Figure out what's most important to you.
- Map out your daily tasks.
- Determine how you want to live your life.
- Talk to a mentor.
- Eliminate distractions.
- Check in with yourself regularly.

Once you have classified all of your activities, hold onto this information. You will use the categories and the items in them to evaluate and organize your schedule on a daily basis. The trick is to find a balance between the urgent and important actions. If you feel overwhelmed with urgencies, try to avoid the items in the last two categories for a few days to free up time and take care of your urgencies. Eventually, the important activities do become urgent when not tended to—so, either way, you will have your opportunity to address them.

Manage Your Time with Determination

You have your priorities, so you know what is important to you. Now it is time apply these ideals to your life. It requires focus and a good portion of determination before it becomes a habit. Right now, with a strategy, your life is chaotic and important activities are slipping right by you, so get to work on you plan:

1. Be PRODUCTIVE, not BUSY by recording the minutes in your day and removing the fluff.
2. PRIORITIZE by creating a list of your activities and placing them in order of importance.
3. CREATE a flexible daily SCHEDULE that considers IMPORTANT and URGENT items.
4. SET short-term GOALS for the next month based on your VALUES.
5. EVALUATE your STRATEGY regularly and make improvements where it is necessary.

MAKING IT HAPPEN!

4 | Money Management

Few things are more rewarding than being the creator of your own destiny, and whether you like it or not, your destiny aligns with your financial situation.

Why is it that some people will not take control of their financial life and create their own destiny? The most common answer is they are afraid. Afraid they will make a mistake. Afraid they will fail. Afraid they're not smart enough. Rest assured, you can take control and eliminate being afraid of anything, including success!

Even financial experts make mistakes along the way. You will too. That should not stop you from tackling the necessary task of managing your money. There is no other choice if you are seeking a secure and sound financial future.

For me, I always believe in spending less than what I earn. And also, invest first, spend later. Many people will take on credit card debts, spending above their means. Accepting your role in your money management comes first. Learning how often to pay attention to what you're money is doing to work for you comes second. Find ways to always produced more than what you spend.

It is important to be mindful of your finances and money every single day. Not just once a week or every other week or monthly—every day!

Simple, proper money management will bring you financial independence, and this individual freedom is a place where you can accomplish all of the things important to you. Far too few people know this place, mostly because they don't take time to learn the skills to succeed at it. If this is your story, I will provide you with the tools to get you off to a great start.

You must consider two things as you move forward with the heartfelt dedication to manage your money properly:

1. Be honest with yourself in identifying what financial independence means to you because it is different for everyone. Take the time to create your own definition. If you are not honest with yourself or you commandeer someone else's definition, your journey will veer from the path and sidetrack you indefinitely.

   Determine what is most important to you, and remember money is only a tool to help you achieve your goals, and not the goal itself.

2. Begin assuming responsibility for your choices and take immediate control of your financial future. Let go of any financial missteps from your past, and step wholeheartedly into today, because today is where you create your destiny and the financial life you deserve. Achieving financial independence stems from the belief you will no longer be at the mercy of whatever life brings you.

   Do not forfeit your power to the universe; instead, use it to make the impossible POSSIBLE. To believe and act otherwise will not get you to where you plan to go.

Achieving Financial Freedom

Every great achievement begins with a dream inspiring desire. Whether there is a direct path to financial freedom or a complex set of steps, three things greatly increase your chances of success:

1. Create an enthusiastic and adaptable attitude about yourself and your ability to make your dreams a reality. You develop an energetic and flexible attitude by building inner confidence about your abilities and maintaining a positive outlook about your future. By remaining positive and earnest through changing situations, you can tackle any situation and remain confident about a satisfying outcome.

*Failure is hardly ever the result of an "inability" to do something,
but an unwillingness to try because of lack of confidence.
Be prepared to accept success.*

2. Commit to doing whatever it takes to make your financial dreams a reality. Dedication to your desired outcomes gives you the strength, agility, and flexibility to overcome or maneuver around obstacles that appear in your path. Without a strong commitment, you might fall prey to the first obstacle that appears, drifting along on a back road leading you astray.

   When times get difficult, and they presumably will at some point, a strong obligation to your financial independence can carry you through to successful completion of your dreams.

3. Use a goal-setting process to develop a systematic approach to accomplishing your desired outcomes. Goal setting provides a structure that enables you to participate actively in turning your financial aspirations into reality.

   You create your own destiny by determining when and how events will happen in your life.

With a positive and enthusiastic attitude, a strong commitment to your financial aspirations, and a plan to accomplish them, you will succeed in turning your dreams into reality.

Establishing Financial Goals

Goals are dreams with deadlines. While goals should have deadlines, they should also include some additional elements not always found in dreams—they should be:

- Specific
- Measurable
- Realistic

MAKING IT HAPPEN!

Begin the process of developing goals by creating statements compiled from a list of your financial aspirations.

Writing down your aspirations helps crystallize your thoughts and brings them into the realm of possibility. Your list may consist of one special desire or many different ones, and it can include dreams for the present or dreams for the future.

Remember to develop aspirations for all of the major areas of your life: personal, family, professional, health, and spiritual, as well as financial. This will keep balance in your life. Try to use all of your senses as you create your dreams… Feel the pride of owning your own business or retiring on your own terms; smell the new car; taste the first meal you cook in your new house; beam with joy as you watch your children graduate from college knowing you were able to help financially. The more senses you use to realize the power of your aspirations, the more real your dreams become.

As you compile your list, also include your reasons for wanting each dream. This statement will bring clarity to what the results of your goal will be when it is reached. Make this statement powerful and compelling, because it will be your inspiration and motivation to keep going until your aspirations becomes a reality.

Next, assign a priority rating to each item on your list. Start with your most important desire first. The process of listing your dreams and prioritizing them is an ongoing task. Plan to repeat it at least once each year or as special events occur in your life. It is normal for your aspirations to change over time. As you grow and change, goals also do. That's why revisions are necessary. You can add new dreams, while updating and/or deleting existing ones. Don't cling to what doesn't serve you well, so long as it isn't really a lack of effort over something no longer right for you.

Once you compile your list, you are ready to convert your dreams to goal statements. Each goal statement should have four basic qualities:

1. **Be specific**
   Paint a picture of your aspirations with words. When your description is complete, what you want to achieve should be crystal clear.

2. Be measurable

Just as you set a destination when you plan a trip, you should include a way to measure the successful completion of your goal. Without this element, you might stop short or keep going longer than you need to, wasting precious time and resources.

3. Include a target completion date

This will keep you on track so you can complete your goals in a timely manner. In addition to a target completion date, build in interim check dates to monitor your progress, so you can make adjustments as needed. Always be aware of your progress—or lack thereof.

4. Be realistic

This can be difficult because it is not always easy to determine what is realistic and what is unrealistic. Sometimes it is obvious, but it can sometimes be much more subtle and have an adverse effect if you are not careful.

Do not put restrictions on your aspirations, but in some cases, you may need to change your approach. If a goal is very important to you, you will find a way to accomplish it. However, if you feel you are stretching yourself too far, here are some options to help keep your sanity while you accomplish your goal:

- **Break your goal into smaller, more manageable pieces**
  This allows you to stack your successes on top of each other until you complete your original goal.

- **Extend the completion date**
  This takes some of the pressure off by allowing more time to complete each step.

- **Take on more risk**
  This could mean making riskier investments with higher potential payouts or taking on projects beyond your comfort zone. Now a word of

caution about this one—make certain you understand and can live with the consequences if things do not work out the way you would like.

- **Put more effort into it**

    For financial goals, this might mean getting a second job or decreasing your expenses. For professional goals, it might mean going back to school or focusing your efforts in one specific area to gain experience or expertise.

Use one or all of these options as much as you can. Be patient (don't abandon a goal too early), yet evaluate often. It is a normal part of the process. We are all constantly changing and evolving in our ideas, our abilities, and our dreams.

The goal statement you develop is the first step you are taking in your goal-setting process. With this step, you are turning your dreams into reality.

Your goal statement is beneficial because it is a clear, concise statement of what you want and why you want it. It shows you've thought things through and are really tapped into what you sense is important. What better motivation to properly manage your money could there be?

A BIT OF ADVICE...

Deciding to accumulate as much money as possible over the next few years is not a goal. It may be a dream, but it's not a complete goal. This sentiment, while nice, is missing some of the essential elements of a goal, such as being specific and measurable. To convert it to a goal, set a specific dollar amount and target date. Then, determine if that amount is realistic for you, given the resources you have available. Remember, with a clear target to aim for, you are more likely to hit it!

Determine Your Needs

Determining your needs is the second step in the goal-setting process. It will create a clear picture of where you are and what you need to accomplish your goals. This step has three components:

1. Determine what is already available to you.
2. Determine what you will need to achieve your goal
3. Determine the gap between what is available and what you need.

Begin by taking an inventory of everything available to assist you in reaching your goals. Depending upon the goal, this may include a financial and/or personal inventory of available assets. Most financial inventories include a cash flow and net worth analysis, while personal inventories include an analysis of assets like education, skills, talents, family, and your network of contacts. Since most goals have a financial component, we will concentrate on how to complete a financial inventory. Later, you can apply these same principles to inventory your personal assets.

A cash flow analysis is a detailed listing of your income and expenses for a specific period, typically a month.

This type of analysis also provides a snapshot of how much money is coming in and where it is going. It shows you at a glance whether you are living within or beyond your means, and the dollars currently available to invest toward your goals. It also provides a starting point to cut expenses or reallocate your dollars if your spending does not match your goals.

In the beginning, you may need to conduct a cash flow analysis more frequently to establish a spending pattern best aligned with your goals; however, once you are comfortable with your spending, you may only need to conduct an analysis once a year to ensure that your spending remains in line with your goals.

MAKING IT HAPPEN!

To get started with your cash flow analysis, gather your bank account, savings account, and credit card statements. Then estimate the amount you spend monthly in each of the following categories:

- Taxes
- Food
- Housing
- Savings and investments
- Insurance
- Medical
- Vehicle expenses and other transportation costs
- Clothing
- Entertainment and recreation
- Miscellaneous

After completing the task of categorizing your expenses, take a look at your bottom line, which is your monthly net cash flow and determine if your expenses are equal to, greater than, or less than your income.

- **Your expenses equal your income**

   This is not a bad situation to be in, especially if you have allotted a portion of your income to the savings and investments category. However, if you are not contributing regularly to an emergency fund or to an investment program, you may have to use charge cards more frequently for unexpected expenses or to make ends meet. If this is the case, look for ways to increase your income or decrease your expenses so you can establish a cash reserve for emergencies. Begin by trimming your expenses in nonessential areas like entertainment. Next, look at essential areas, like housing, to determine ways to trim costs. If you do nothing, you could easily fall into the next category.

- **Your expenses are greater than your income**

   If you fall into this category and it is not a temporary condition, you must find ways to cut back on your spending and/or increase your income immediately. Continuing to live beyond your means makes it impossible to invest toward your goals now, and it jeopardizes your ability to do so in the future. As you work your way out of this situation, build a cash reserve. This will help you maintain a positive position.

- **Your expenses are less than your income**
  Congratulations! You are off to a good start. You have money available to start or continue an investment program to help you achieve your goals. However, if you do not have a cash reserve in place, begin a special fund immediately.

Next, continue your financial inventory with a net worth analysis. You calculate your net worth by subtracting your liabilities – the things you owe – from your assets, which are the things you own.

You use a net worth analysis for the following reasons:

- To uncover assets you have available to assist you in reaching your goals
- To estimate your retirement income
- To determine your estate and insurance needs
- To serve as a base or reference point for evaluating your progress toward your financial independence

Plan to calculate your net worth annually. Or sooner if you have a major change in your life.

The process of calculating your net worth will go faster if you organize your important papers before you start. Gather all of your documents and statements relating to your assets and liabilities. You will need to know the value of your assets and the balance on your liabilities. In the case of appreciating assets, like your home, you may need to do some research to determine the current market value. Local realtors are a good place to start for home values and the Internet is a good source for current auto values.

As you work toward your goals, your net worth should increase. If it does not, this may be an indication that your liabilities are growing faster than your assets. The key to increasing your net worth is to increase your assets. In other words, purchase more assets or hold assets that appreciate, and decrease your liabilities, which are your debts, or a combination of these things.

What You Need to Reach Your Goal

The next step is to determine what you will need to have happen and/or how much money you will need to complete your goal. Since everyone's situation is unique, it is impossible to generalize about what it will take to accomplish your goals. But this is what works for me; if you do not already have an idea of what it will take, do some research. There are a number of resources available to assist you, including:

- Libraries
- Professionals who work in the area of your goal
- Colleagues
- Business contacts
- Community agencies
- Internet searching (from reliable sources)

If you research, and it is still not possible to develop a good estimate of what it will take to accomplish your goal, make your best guess from the information you have gathered and move on. Do not let this piece stop you from moving forward. Instead, start working toward your goal and plan to make adjustments as more information becomes available.

Closing the Gap

"The gap" represents the difference between what you have available to assist you in achieving your goals and what you need to accomplish them. The gap may be in the form of extra dollars needed to complete a goal, like a down payment on a house, strategies to allocate current dollars to provide an ongoing stream of income for a goal like retirement, or strategies to protect your investments in order to maintain their current value.

Remember, not all gaps are related to a shortage of dollars; they may surface due to the wrong financial allocations in your current plan. To determine the gap you need to fill, subtract what you have available from what you need to complete your goal. That number is your gap.

Congratulations! You now know where you are, where you want to go, and what it will take to get there. I realize that this step of the goal-setting process takes some time to complete, but it is well worth the effort. Without the foundation this step provides, you might be missing vital information needed to work for your benefit in creating the financial future you deserve. You have now passed one major milestone and you are definitely moving forward on the road to financial independence. Way to go!

Develop a Financial Plan

Developing a plan to reach financial independence is the third step in the goal-setting process. The result of this step is to create a specific map you can follow to make your aspirations a reality. However, before you create your plan, it is important to consider the effects of two major forces—compounding and inflation. The longer your timeframe, the more dramatic the effect of these forces, and the greater the necessity to adjust your plan to ensure that you will have what you need when it is time to complete your goal.

Compounding is the positive force working for your money.

Albert Einstein once called compounding, or the process of earning interest on your interest, the eighth wonder of the world. While on the surface this may sound too simple to generate such high praise from someone like Einstein, the effect it can have on your investments is nothing less than remarkable. Einstein recognized this. Now you do too!

Compounding causes your investments to grow at an accelerating rate each year, and it does this whether or not you continue to add to them. Over time, the results can be astounding.

For example, if you place $2,000 in an account that pays 10 percent interest each year, at the end of the first year you will have $2,200, which is the $2,000 you started with plus $200 interest. If you make no withdrawals or deposits to this account, at the end of the second year you will have $2,420, which is $2,200 plus $220 interest. As long as you keep your money invested, this process will repeat itself each year. After thirty years, your account will total almost $35,000, all from your original $2,000 investment. That is the power of compounding plus time.

If we take the above example a step further, and in addition to allowing your dollars to grow over time, you add to your account on a regular basis, you will increase the effects of compounding even more. For example, if you add $2,000 each year, in thirty years your account will total more than $360,000 from a $60,000 investment—the result of compounding plus time plus a consistent investment program. To take full advantage of compounding, invest your dollars as early in the year as possible.

Inflation is the positive force working against your money.

Inflation gradually increases the cost of goods and services that you use. Inflation influences almost everything, from items you purchase frequently like bread, milk, and gasoline, to items you purchase less frequently, like houses, cars, and appliances. However, they are not all affected by inflation in the same way. Some will increase at a rate less than or equal to inflation, while others will increase at a rate greater than inflation.

For example, if annual inflation rates have averaged 2 to 3 percent for the past decade, increases in college costs may inflate to 6 to 7 percent. Although inflation may have only a mild effect on what you will need for short-term goals, it can have a dramatic effect on mid-term and long-term goals. Always consider the effects of inflation when determining what you will need to achieve your goals. Make adjustments, if necessary, to ensure their successful completion.

Why is it so important to make adjustments for inflation? Remember, inflation is like compounding—the effects add on each year. If inflation averages 3.5 percent, an annual pension of $30,000 today would buy goods and services worth only $21,268 in ten years and $15,077 in twenty years. In other words, twenty years into retirement, inflation could cut your pension and your standard of living by fifty percent.

While the details of everyone's financial goals may be different, the process of determining what you will need to do to accomplish them, determining the gap, and making adjustments for compounding and inflation is the same for everyone.

Overcoming the Obstacles to Your Financial Goals

Identifying obstacles you could encounter and developing methods to overcome them is the last step in the goal-setting process. Obstacles are generally a part of the process of goal achievement and how you deal with them may mean the difference between successfully completing your goals or not.

Obstacles may be in the form of small nuisances easily overcome, or they may be so horrendous they seriously jeopardize your chances of ever achieving your goals. This is why a checks and balances system is important. It will help you stay on track—or quickly get back on track if you find yourself derailed.

For financial goals, there are two basic types of obstacles you are likely to encounter:

1. Obstacles related to your underlying attitudes and beliefs
2. Obstacles resulting from an internal or external conflict

Obstacles related to your internal system of attitudes and beliefs are powerful. They can be good or bad, and often times you are unaware of their existence. This gives them the potential to sabotage you or skyrocket you to achievement.

Some attitudes and beliefs that are particularly hazardous to your financial health include:

- **You believe money is the root of evil**
  Many people hear this statement and consciously or unconsciously use it to sabotage their efforts to create a successful financial life. Remember, money is a tool to help you achieve your goals, and you do not need to love it to put it to work for you. You should not feel guilt about earning it and having it either.

MAKING IT HAPPEN!

- **You become a victim of procrastination**
  Stop saying, "As soon as I get comfortable in my job, I will start saving," or "As soon as I get out of debt, I will start saving," or "As soon as the kids get in school, I can start saving." Excuses can be never-ending. Procrastination becomes a hazard to your financial health when it stops you from achieving your goals. The truth is most people never get EVERYTHING in order because life is not static; it is constantly changing. If you wait for the perfect day to come, you will never get started.

- **You believe something or someone will come along to rescue you**
  Maybe you will marry a millionaire, win the lottery, receive an inheritance, or find a briefcase full of money, but that's hardly a guarantee, right? Instead of waiting for these things to happen to you – which is unlikely – prepare a financially secure future for yourself, so you will always have security and reach your goals in a timely manner.

To overcome these obstacles and others, you must believe in yourself and your abilities. You must believe you deserve the things you want in your life, and you must be willing to accept responsibility to do whatever it takes to make it happen.

If your attitudes and beliefs are making it difficult for you to achieve your goals, it may be possible to work on them until you regain control by using one or more of the following methods:

- **Place reminders about your goal where you can see them each day**
  A note or picture on your bathroom mirror or your refrigerator can work wonders. This gives you the opportunity to focus on your goals daily, making them a part of your everyday life.

- **Set up programs requiring little or no effort on your part**
  For example, if saving is difficult, consider automatic transfers from your checking account into your favorite mutual fund, or participating in a savings plans through work. In other words, put as much of your plan as possible on autopilot until you can take over.

- **Break your goal into smaller units to see results more quickly**
  These smaller successes help you build your enthusiasm and motivation to continue until the goal is complete.

By fixing your attitude and belief system about money, you grow into a person better able to manage conflict-related obstacles when they surface. Typically, these stem from three general areas:

1. Internal conflict or a disharmony with your internal value system
2. External conflicts with others and their goals
3. Internal and external conflicts created by a lack of adequate planning

The results of these conflicts can range from mild anxiety to total abandonment of your goals. As soon as you determine you have a conflict situation, for the sake of your goal, take steps to resolve it as soon as possible. In many cases, these obstacles are a combination of two or more types of conflict, and if you do not know what you are looking for, they may not be easy to recognize. Here are some common obstacles:

- **You may occasionally find yourself listening to other people and adopting their dreams as your own**
  Sometimes this works, but more often it creates conflict. As you work toward the goal, you may begin to resent making sacrifices and spending your precious time working on a goal that was never really yours. Unfortunately, this insight usually occurs after you have expended a lot of energy and resources, and the thought of throwing it all away may be just as painful as continuing to work toward the goal. Now, the goal is no longer a dream, but a chore. Nobody wants this!

  Take the time to explore your inner self and dream your own dreams. Keep expanding your horizons until you create your own vision.

- **Seeing a situation from completely different perspective than family, leading to struggles**
  If you're constantly fighting an uphill battle, you risk big difficulties in accomplishing even an easily attainable goal. There is no joy in the process. Therefore, include everyone who can influence your success in the process.

  Share your goals, try to determine as many sources of family conflicts as possible, and take steps to resolve them before they become major obstacles.

- **You set too many goals or set unrealistic timeframes**
  If this happens and things begin to fall apart, go back to the planning phase. Remember, it may not always be possible to accomplish everything at once, and even if you could, it may not be your best option, especially if it is at the expense of taking time to celebrate your victories. An important part of accomplishing goals is acknowledging the joy of completion.

  Celebrating your successes compounds your enthusiasm and motivation, and it recharges your batteries for the next challenge.

As you work toward your goals, obstacles can surface at any time. Planning for them can greatly enhance your chances of overcoming or maneuvering around them so you remain on track. You know yourself best, which is why only you can determine what your financial goals are. Only you can recognize potential obstacles. Once you do, face those obstacles head-on—deal with them so you can move past them.

Your 10-Point Personal Strategy Checklist

Use this checklist to make sure you're taking action toward money management goals. They are a must in your pursuits of securing your financial destiny.

1. Be proactive
Starting today, take responsibility and control of your financial future. Develop a positive attitude and inner confidence about your abilities to manage your future.

2. Make a strong commitment to your aspirations
A strong commitment gives you the strength, flexibility, and agility to overcome and/or maneuver around obstacles appearing in your path. This is usually necessary when you are seeing a goal to completion.

3. Use the goal-setting process to convert your dreams into goals
You take control when you convert your dreams into goals. You determine when and how things will happen in your life. Formulate your goals to be specific, measurable, and realistic. Also, include a target completion date.

4. Do your homework!
Determine your current financial condition, what you will need to do in order to accomplish your goals, and identify any gaps you need to fill. Then develop a systematic plan to make your dream a reality.

5. Adjust your plan for the effects of inflation
Over time, inflation erodes your purchasing power. While it may have only a mild effect on short-term goals, it can have a dramatic effect on the amount of money you will need for long-term goals like retirement. As you develop your plan, always consider the effects of inflation and make adjustments if necessary.

6. Take advantage of compounding plus time
Compounding is the process of earning interest on your interest. Compounding plus time can greatly accelerate the growth of your investments. The earlier you start the greater the effect will be, but it is never too late to start.

7. Monitor your progress

Set interim check dates to compare your actual progress to your plan. Make adjustments if necessary to stay on track.

8. Focus on your goals daily

What you focus on, you tend to follow. Set up daily, weekly, monthly, and annual activities to accomplish your goals, and get started. The best day to have started working toward your goals was yesterday. The next best day is today!

9. Anticipate obstacles

You cannot anticipate every obstacle, but if you take time to consider some common stumbling blocks and practice how you will react when you encounter them, you can greatly increase your chances of recovering quickly and getting back on track to achieve your goals. As your troubleshooting skills increase, so will your confidence in your ability to make your dreams a reality.

10. Educate yourself

Since you cannot possibly learn everything you need to know about achieving financial independence in one day, establish a time each day, week, or month to educate yourself. Read books, newspapers, and magazines, attend seminars, and participate in activities to continue your financial education.

If you occasionally fall – and we all do – do not let that stop you from achieving your goal. Keep progressing and pursuing it. There is great dignity in this and it feels rewarding. Once you achieve one goal, take a deep breath, pat yourself on the back, and start the process all over again. Never stop dreaming!

5 | How to Start a Business

"A journey of a thousand miles begins with a single step."
— **Lao Tzu**

For many years now, companies have become less loyal to their employees. This trend escalated after the 2008 economic crash and all the company downsizing and employee layoffs resulting from it. To make the sting worse for employees, their benefits have seen a decline over the years. What was once offered is no longer is for a myriad of reasons. One of the biggest is a company can make an employee part-time and avoid paying a great many benefits. Now, they may have to do this to keep afloat, but that still doesn't change the shifting dynamics the employee has to deal with.

Competition has also factored into corporate cultures. There is so much of it and to remain competitive – a/k/a keep costs down – contract employees have become more commonplace. This most often takes place in the form of:

- Outsourcing work to third world countries with extremely low labor costs
- Benefiting from freelance employees for specific task

The one thing outsourcing and freelancing have in common—a business doesn't pay benefits on them.

With all this going on, no wonder things feel so tough for so many people. But within that toughness a tremendous opportunity to start your own business exists. This has become an increasingly popular and desirable option for many. The biggest problem of doing this is most businesses startups also fail within the first five years. Then the numbers decrease again at the ten-year and fifteen-year marks.

If you've got an idea and a vision, you need to ask yourself some tough questions and be brutally honest with the answers.

- How can you make sure your business idea will make it?
- How do you even go about starting your own business?

Let's dive in, shall we?

Big Companies that Started in a Garage

First, let's amp up your desire!

What do Google, Apple, Microsoft, Amazon, Disney, and Hewlett-Packard all have in common? They all started in a garage! You see, you don't build the building and then craft the business, you craft the business so you can progress to the building—or whatever other type of space you need to succeed in your business environment.

> *The thing to understand is most of these mega business moguls had zero idea they were going to grow multi-billion dollar companies.*

Sure, they saw themselves as having a good idea and they were filled with a need. But most of them didn't realize just how big and successful they were going to become. They didn't cap their limit, but they had no idea how far it would go.

Take this concept to heart in your life—it serves as an excellent reminder about how your humble beginnings are no indication of the success you may have. Everyone starts at the base level – an idea – and builds it up from there.

So, let's discuss what you need to do before you lay even one brick, or even create your business name...

Analyze the Market

The first thing you should do before anything else is to analyze the market your business will serve. You must figure out:

- Who your customer is
- What age group they are
- What do they dislike
- What do they complain about

And most importantly...

- How are your competitors NOT serving them properly right now?

Typically, you must figure out how your business will be better than the competition. Can you offer your customers greater value for the same price or less? It doesn't matter how superior your concept may be to what's out there, nowadays with Google and other search engines, consumers do a lot of research. As for you—you also need these resources for your own thorough analysis of your market.

Other areas you should seek input from include forums and social media sites like Facebook, Twitter, Instagram or Pinterest. Study what people say about your competition. Many of your answers for offering solutions to peoples' problems lie right there.

Investopedia published an article titled, *Top 6 Reasons New Businesses Fail* (https://www.investopedia.com/slide-show/top-6-reasons-new-businesses-fail), and one of the main reasons for failure is because the business owner didn't investigate the market before they started. What a costly mistake!

It's really quite simple and logical. You have to figure out if there is a high demand for what you want to offer, and you have to make sure the market is not saturated with companies who already have the service for said industry. This leads to a key component, which must be a part of your business from the moment you start conceptualizing it.

Why You Must Love Your Customer

If money is your motivation to start a business, you are starting with the wrong motivation.

Too many businesses were started with money motivation. Today, that doesn't work. The competition is great enough that you must love your customer. If you don't, your competitors will—and do so authentically because they had the proper motivation.

Customers love to feel the businesses they interact with really do care about them. If they sense they are not cared for, and there is any other option out there, they will seek it out. If there is no other option out there, someone with the right insights will spot the demand for "better" and pursue it with a customer-centric focus.

You can't even keep bad customer service quiet anymore due to online reviews. Anyone can rate you and your company. Even Google does it with the 5-star system. Amazon does it... Trip Advisor does it. And Yelp is another business feedback platform where any company can be scrutinized under the watchful eyes of customers… And, the brutal truth is many customers are downright unfair. A business may have done nothing wrong, but a customer was disappointed for whatever reason and they unleash their fury out into the digital world. Unfortunate situations happen even to great businesses, but the strategies for your survival fall into how you manage your customer after those moments.

This begs the questions: 1) Could you love your customer? 2) Can you see yourself serving them fully from a place of love?

Another question is: do you have the passion and the interest in your business for constant improvement? You need to! Your business is like a tree... If it's not growing, it's dying. You have to be happy with the idea of improving every aspect of your business in every way from the moment you start it.

Big questions, big evaluations. What are you going to do?

Do You Really Have the Dedication and Time?

Most new business owners don't realize one thing—a business owner is a business owner 24 hours a day, 7 days a week, for 365 days a year... At first, it will feel like the ones who have it easy are the employees!

Owning your own business is not anything like a job where when you put in your time, go home, and then forget about work until the next morning when you're back at it.

When you have a job, typically, you are off on the weekends. Normally, you don't even have to think about work at all. Your time off is YOUR time...

Then you pursue the dream of starting your own business and everything changes.

- Are you going to be okay with working around the clock sometimes?
- Are you sure you have the dedication, the motivation, and the passion to work on your business full time with no break for a while?

You had better know – and believe with absolute conviction – you can take what is involved with being a business owner. Sure, after the business starts succeeding, you will be able to take some time off. But until then, don't kid yourself. It can take non-stop action for weeks, months, and even years to get a business to the point where you have true time freedom.

What keeps you going during these times? It's your customers and your love of what you do to help them while becoming successful.

If you're not here quite yet, relax. You can amp up your thoughts and practices to prepare yourself to become a successful business owner.

Develop a New Attitude

"It's not the lack of resources, it's your lack of resourcefulness that stops you."
— **Tony Robbins**

Here are some more questions you need to ask yourself before deciding to start a new business…

- Are you willing to do whatever it takes to succeed?
- Or are you the type who gets too easily discouraged once things start to get a little difficult?

The problem for most wanna-be business owners is once they get into the nitty-gritty of the business, they lose their passion. They get easily discouraged. Dreaming is exciting and many required actions are not.

In order to become a successful businessperson you must develop a new attitude. You must determine beforehand that whatever problem comes up, you'll be able to solve it. Whatever happens, you will handle it. And if you can't handle it in the moment, then you'll figure it out…

Although it's not a statistic, you could find many businesses have failed due to a flailing attitude. If your attitude needs adjusting, get to work! You have to develop a new attitude that you are capable of doing what it takes, and appreciative of even the roughest parts of the journey.

Only you can determine if you will not allow any circumstance, person or event to get you down, relative to your business.

And guess what? It's okay if you don't know all the answers. There is a plethora of free or low-cost help available to help business start-ups. Use the internet; research your problems and see if you can find solutions that have worked for those problems with other business owners. Read books, find a mentor, and continually invest good energy in creating a great business.

Decide right now that you're not going to let ANYTHING stop you from becoming successful.

With this attitude, you will do what one of Tony Robbins books said to do, which is to awaken the giant within...

Make a Smooth Transition

Few people can go "all in" when they start a new business—at least not time wise. Perhaps you are working a 9-to-5 job right now, dreaming about starting your own business... Perhaps you know that it's going to be very successful... Perhaps you have done all of the market research, you know your customers, you know your competition, and the future looks really good for you...

This is all great, of course, but what should you do now? That's what you need to know!

Should you quit your job and dive right in? Typically, the answer is "no." Why? Because it's too risky.

Business is risky. Your job is not. If you quit your day job to start your business and it fails, you could end up in financial ruin. You could get your house foreclosed on, or not be able to pay rent. The stress you would go through could easily become almost unbearable. Your health could suffer, and all of your relationships too. Nothing I just described is worth the risk!

If you have a job now, the best way to start a business is gradually. There is no need to add additional stress as you begin the process of learning what you need to know. There is so much information, so why not go slowly and really learn it?

When your business income exceeds your job income, then you can quit your job. What you are looking for is stability in your business before you quit.

If your situation is different and you have the ability to create your business without needing a job to survive, then great. You don't have to worry about it as much. But if you do have a job, the best way to transition into your business is to wait until it is making what your job is making.

How to Take Your Ideas from Mind to Market to Profit

Your mind is a powerful tool and your greatest business asset. There is one other asset you have and may have overlooked—your intuition.

Have you ever had the circumstance happen where you didn't trust your gut instinct? We all have, of course! When we don't trust our intuition, we almost always regret it…

I think being mindful of intuition's role in your life can answer some of the most perplexing questions out there about business…

- Why is it that some people thrive in business and some don't?
- Why is it that some very intelligent people can fail in business, while others who are not as smart succeed?

The answer is simple—intuition. It helps with success in all areas of your life, and definitely in business!

Your intuition will never steer you wrong. And the sooner that you realize that, the better…

Go with your gut. Sometimes the people who go with their gut instinct instead of statistics and analysis end up taking risks and thriving. It may seem contradictory—in one sense you should do all of this research and analysis before starting your business, and on the other, go with your gut instinct. The trick is to be balanced with both.

If you can, do the research. But use your gut instinct as the final decision maker.

To Market We Go

You've got the idea and now it's time to go to the market. It is both smart and insightful to test the market out so you can see if people want what you plan to offer. You could get the opinions from friends and relatives, but be a bit cautious with this approach. Some friends and relatives may be a little jealous you are starting a new business. Or, they may be afraid to give you impartial and valuable feedback. It happens and it can be challenging to be honest with someone you care about—even if it isn't doing you a service as a budding entrepreneur.

You are also going to have to figure out what business name to create, how to brand yourself, your business logo, and email marketing. Email is so important in today's business culture. One huge mistake many businesses make is that they don't capture the email addresses of their customers when they start up. Don't make that mistake! Every single email address that you can capture is golden; especially if it is a customer who has already done business with you.

Going to market requires proper business creation in many areas, including:

- Branding
- Creating a unique selling proposition
- Identifying your niche market
- Figuring out what your startup costs will be

Let's cover these now.

Branding

Think of branding from the perspective of when a cowboy brands his cow. It has to be a unique identifier easily seen and understood by others.

Branding is your way to identify who you are to the world. Taking that a step further, it also should evoke a feeling. When you think of the brand "Coca-Cola," they want you to feel the feeling of refreshment—have a Coke and a smile. When you think of the brand "Apple," they want you to feel the ease of using their product and instantly connect with its high quality. The "McDonalds" brand wants you to feel the feeling of fun. It has little to do with the quality of their hamburgers!

Unique Selling Proposition

Your USP is important. It will be in all of your marketing materials.

Usually, you have to have a unique selling proposition (or point) in order to be competitive. Can you offer something of more value than your competitors? Or can you offer something that costs less but is of the same value?

Identifying Your Niche Market

Identifying a market niche is one of the greatest challenges for new business owners to understand. Why? The main reason is the belief you can serve anyone often exists. Turn business away? No way!

If you try to serve everyone, then you serve no one.

Here's a good way to illustrate this…

Imagine you have a heart problem. Which doctor would you prefer to go to? A general practitioner who serves everyone, or a heart specialist? A cardiologist? You would want the one who SPECIALIZES in the problem that you have. Nothing else would be logical in that situation.

With the internet, we no longer have to worry nearly as much about finding enough people to serve. We can literally find thousands of customers rather easily.

So, don't be afraid to specialize. The more you specialize, the more your right customers will know you are the right business for them.

Startup Costs

You will need to figure out how much you will need to start up your business. Brick and mortar businesses are costly. But internet based businesses are not.

Can you work from home? How much will it be to rent an office where you live? These are the things you will need to consider. Whichever route you choose, you will need to find out the real cost. This can be a difficult task. There can be a lot of hidden costs to starting up a business, so it's always best to have more than what you think you will need.

You will also want to open up a business bank account and decide if you want to hire an accountant to manage your books. If you're not a fan of complete organization of paperwork, you may want to consider becoming a fan of a good and reliable accountant. They can help with taxes, payroll, and a slew of other important things you must be mindful of.

With a sound feel for what you need to do before you even start, if you want to start your business, great! You probably have what it takes to be an entrepreneur.

But if all of this sounds like too much trouble and work, then maybe starting a business is not a good idea for you right now... Either way, you might as well learn some information about it and take advantage of this resource to help you create a strategy if you ever do become ready!

Collaboration and Cooperation Versus Competition

Cooperation and collaboration are starting to replace competition.

There is a new trend in the world of business. It's subtle. It's not that apparent in many ways. And most don't see it at all. What is it? It's collaboration instead of competition; and it's cooperation instead of competition.

Increasingly more companies and small business owners are realizing that once they are fairly well established, cooperating with other business owners might be better than competing. The way it works is if one business owner has a unique product or service they may ask another business owner – one who has a large email list – if they can cooperate together.

How?

They can go into a business deal where they both get 50/50 profit from it. In this case, the product or service from one business owner (who may be new and not have a list) can be sent to the large email list of the other business owner and they both make money. Usually in this case, the business owner with the big list really has to evaluate the risk of doing this "cross-promotion" deal. The product or service must be different, and it must be something that the customers would want.

> *One way cooperation is effective is if both the young generation, who are on top of the social media game, and the older generation, who have more experience, work together. By cooperating together, they can form strong alliances where both of their strengths can be used.*

For example, if an older business owner has a well-matured product or service, he or she may use the services of a younger business partner who knows how to market using social media. The younger generation can benefit from the older ones wisdom and experience, and the older generation can benefit from the younger ones knowledge of social media.

Short To-Do-List

"The graveyard is the richest place on earth, because it is here that you will find all the hopes and dreams that were never fulfilled, the books that were never written, the songs that were never sung, the inventions that were never shared, the cures that were never discovered, all because someone was too afraid to take that first step, keep with the problem, or determined to carry out their dream."
— Les Brown

If you are going to start your own business, you have to get comfortable with Googling information. A quick search on "How to Start a Business" on Google will show an article by Jeff Haden titled, "How to Start a Small Business in a Few Hours." The article describes how Jeff had a neighbor who constantly talked about how he wanted to start up his own business. After the neighbor mentioning this for over six months, Jeff got fed up. He challenged his neighbor to start up his business. Jeff bet his neighbor lunch that they could set up his business in under three hours… He succeeded… Please note that this is the administrative part. This does not include creating a business plan.

It's still a start and it is rewarding!

Step 1: Get over the company name thing
Many people agonize over details such as what to name their company. Meanwhile, they are delaying making any money! So, don't waste too much time deciding what to name your company. You can change it in the future. Choose a name and go for it…

Step 2: Get an Employer Identification Number (EIN)
An EIN number is used by the IRS to identify your business. It's free. You don't really need one unless you start an LLC or a corporation, but getting

one now means you won't have to use your personal Social Security Number. The benefit to using an EIN number instead of a SSN number is you won't be as susceptible to identity theft.

Step 3: Register your trade name
If you choose to have a business name, you may have to register a trade name. You will have to research this to find out the law for where you live… Usually this is easy to do.

Step 4: Get your business license
Your city or county will likely require you to have a business license (it depends on business). Usually there is a small fee. Make sure to use your EIN number instead of your SSN number.

Step 5: Complete a Business Personal Property Tax Form (if necessary)
Check out your local law for this. Items such as machinery or computers used for your business may be subject to property taxes. Uncle Sam likes to tax everything!

Step 6: Find out if you need other permits
Ask your locality about other permits. There may be zoning issues if you work out of your house.

Step 7: Get a Certificate of Resale (if necessary)
According to the Haden article, "A certificate of resale, also known as a seller's permit, allows you to collect state sales tax on products sold. There is no sales tax on services. You can visit your state department's taxation's website for more details.

Step 8: Get a business bank account
It's very important to keep your business transactions away from your personal transactions. The IRS will slap your hand hard if you comingle funds. Use your EIN number with your bank account in order to keep your personal and business accounts separate.

Step 9: Setup a simple accounting system
At first, you won't have any revenue to report. So, keep a simple Excel spreadsheet or something equivalent in order to keep track of your revenue and expenses. Later, you can invest your time, energy, and money to learning Quickbooks or whatever software you want…

***

In summary, starting a business can be one of the most rewarding experiences you will ever have. That doesn't mean it won't be difficult though! Or possibly a losing proposition. This should make you cautious, but not stop you if you have an idea you truly love. Just remember, if you love your customers, you will have an edge. Inspired action won't feel like hard work. When you do what you love, time flies and you'll feel energized and happy… You have an attitude designed for success, and that, my friend, is something you can take to the bank!

MAKING IT HAPPEN!

6 | Leadership

"You can buy people's time; you can buy their physical presence at a given place; you can even buy a measured number of muscular motions per hour. But you cannot buy enthusiasm... you cannot buy loyalty... you cannot buy the devotion of their hearts. This you must earn."
— **Clarence Francis, Chairman of General Foods**

This quote above was spoken by Clarence Francis shortly after the end of World War II. Despite this, it's only relatively recently that people have actually applied the quotes profound wisdom. In the history of man, leaders have always existed, leaving a legacy for those who came after them. Some leaders leave a legacy of prosperity and power, others a legacy of war and destruction. Be it powerful and significant, or challenging or horrible, the legacy a leader passes on to the next generation leaves an indelible mark on how history views them.

You only have to look at Abraham Lincoln and Adolf Hitler to see the stark contrast of leadership par excellence and leadership that took the wrong turn. And more often than not, history cannot be rewritten unless you are some kind of a Marcos, whose family will do everything within their power and resources to clear your name.

Running a business is a microcosm of running a nation. If you are to succeed in your business, you have to be first, a leader. Not just a leader by name, but a leader by action—an individual who understands the implication of their actions on the word.

What is True Leadership?

The common misconception about leadership is that it is a position of power, influence, and money—a way to gain privilege and honor. For many, being a leader has something to do with recognition, an accomplishment of some sort, an entitlement. The result of this flawed thinking is we see a lot of "leaders" who abuse their positions because of greed and power. We've seen what personal ambition can do. It has the potential to plunge their nation into mediocrity instead of greatness. Most politicians spend more time and effort to keep their power instead of getting things done. This also takes place in the business arena.

In business, present day leaders exploit their subordinates to gain much from them while offering little. These leaders don't care about the welfare of those who work for them, choosing to treat their employees as liabilities, an expense that needs to be reduced in order to gain more profit. There's a reason why most executives are called managers instead of leaders: managers tell people what to do, while leaders inspire their people to do what needs to be done by words and example.

"Leadership is not about titles, positions or flowcharts. It is about one life influencing another."
– John C. Maxwell

How about you? How do you want to be perceived as a leader, and what is the legacy that you want to leave behind?

7 Reasons Why Leadership is Crucial to the Success of a Business

Behind every organization's or business' success stands a strong leader. In the absence of a leader, a company's resources – no matter how vast – cannot work together effectively.

The leader is essential because:

1. A leader is a catalyst
In any organization, the leader is the person who ignites action in others. True leaders don't make followers out of people. Rather, they make leaders out of them.

"If you want to go fast, go alone. If you want to go far, go together."
— **Traditional African Proverb**

---

2. A leader is a morale booster
No one else can build morale like true leaders do. When staff morale is down, your business bears the cost of low productivity, performance, and creativity. When your staff is happy, they stop working for the money alone. This means they start enjoying and loving what they do. As a result, you get better quality of work, lesser leave of absences, and increased output.

3. A leader is a confidence builder
Confident employees make positive contributions, yield a high level of productivity, and create solutions to problems more efficiently. If you show confidence in your workers, they will gain more confidence in their abilities.

4. A leader provides a pleasant work environment

Work is not often fun or enjoyable. Providing a great place for your staff is crucial for their mental and emotional health. Happy employees can do great and amazing things, and bring enormous benefits to the company.

5. A leader points the way

The vision of a leader manifests in the beliefs, values, goals, and actions of the staff. For an organization to succeed, everyone involved should be looking and moving in the same direction at roughly the same pace.

6. A leader motivates

The right motivation comes from influence. A good leader keeps his team motivated through thick and thin by giving them something to believe in deeply. Once your staff finds meaning in what they do, your organization is poised for success.

7. A leader inspires

Inspiration is the source of creativity. It opens the eyes of your people to a better perspective, set conscious goals, and enables them to transcend their limitations.

These are great in theory, but easier said than done, right? You're absolutely correct! If everyone business leader understood principles, all businesses would be successful.

Now the foundation has been laid; what happens next? These principles need to be applied. This is how a leader effectively builds, boosts, inspires, motivates, leads, creates, and ignites action.

The Greatest Leader of All Time

By all standards, he failed as a leader. The man who healed many, walked on the surface of the sea, and calmed the storm could not even extricate himself from the cross that was holding him hostage. He was so fearless that he challenged the authority of the governing body; he was so powerful that people wanted to install him as king. Yet he was so weak that he could not even utter a single word to defend himself from the false accusations hurled against him. In the end, he was betrayed—many of his followers deserted him and many of them even shouted, "Crucify him!"

But that single display of weakness, which was once regarded as foolishness, became the wisest act of all in the most well lived life of any man. Presently, that weak man has more than 2 billion living adherents, and in a span of 2,000 years, more than 70 million believers willingly followed his lead to die for him. Call them stupid, fools, or morons, still the truth remains: a man "who died for them" inspired many people to "die for him" in return. Talk about leadership.

Putting religion and spirituality aside, Jesus Christ is perhaps the greatest leader who ever lived. No one in the history of man has been discussed more, worshipped more, the subject of more debates, books, songs, and artworks. And no other historical figure that was tried, tortured, and executed as a criminal emerged as a more revered personality—ever. By the way, he won back the support of his followers—including their all-out love and willingness to give their lives for his cause. We can surely learn a lesson or two from him on leadership.

Too few businessmen consider Jesus the epitome of a leader. Why, if they were to follow him to the letter, they would probably end up giving all they have to the poor and everything they have worked for would just go down the drain. Worse, they may end up dead, as all the other martyrs.

But believe it or not, incredible people have become great leaders and successful entrepreneurs by following the Christ's leadership example, whether consciously or unconsciously. These qualities exist in "legendary" leaders such as George Washington, Thomas Jefferson, and Abraham Lincoln, all who saw and emulated Jesus in some manner.

8 Secrets of a Great Leadership

The secret's out, I guess. With these bits of wisdom, may you develop the leader in you so that you may leave your amazing mark on this world.

   1. **Great leadership is an inside job**
   Before Jesus set out to change the world, he worked on himself first. A leader can only go as far as his character takes him, so if you aspire to be a leader, you have to start from the inside out. Jesus' pure heart and unfailing character may be a hard act to follow, but keeping your integrity intact cannot hurt. As a business leader, you are morally obligated to use ethical means to achieve your goals; to make your business contribute to the greatest good for the greatest number. You can do this and turn a profit through providing a fair exchange of value for the services rendered by your people.

   > *A great leader must exhibit altruism and must not be self-serving. If you adhere to a certain set of values and principles, and choose to do the right thing even when no one is looking, you will gain the respect, trust, and faith of your people.*

   Once your people believe in you, they cease to be mere employees. They become your followers.

   2. **Great leadership has a compelling vision**
   Jesus clearly outlined his vision: a place where there will be no more weeping, no hurt or pain, no sickness, no suffering, no war, no fear, no death. This may sound preposterous, but Jesus was certainly providing solutions to man's deepest needs. In the same manner, businesses are here to provide solutions for day-to-day problems and satisfy market needs. You may not be a visionary, but do not allow this to keep you from finding a problem, examining its root cause, and creating a breakthrough solution. Find a crisis and a solution that goes beyond today, and then present a picture of a future better than the present, something that would create a real and lasting change. Voila, you have your vision!

One example is the problem of today's non-biodegradable wastes. It's a huge concern for everyone. Envision a plastic-free world, back it with a workable master plan, define the steps to achieve it, and you will win a lot of people on your side. It's a worthy cause to champion. A majority in most communities would partake in this vision.

> *As a leader, you need to have that imagination, insight, and boldness to bring the best out of your people and give them a profound sense of purpose.*

If you want to be a great leader, find a vision that is big enough to move, and inspire people. This is a vision larger than you, and a leader must have one.

3. Great leadership inspires

The root word for inspiration is "spirit," so if one inspires people it means he gifts his followers with his spirit. Jesus certainly did that, albeit supernaturally. Centuries later, in the stark absence of supernatural endowment, the spirit of enthusiasm and determination to spread his teachings still burn fiercely within the hearts of Jesus' followers. Why? Because Jesus' words are so powerful they continue to set people on fire. Would you believe that you are capable of placing your spirit in your followers' hearts and setting them on fire with energy and passion? You are!

Present day leaders ignite the fires of potential through their spirit. Placing your spirit within a person is simply the act of influencing their thoughts, feelings, and behaviors. Today's influencers are the shamans of yesterday. People like Oprah, Tony Robbins, Robert Kiyosaki, and even lesser known individuals share their spirit with others daily.

> *We've seen that a lot with celebrities and charismatic leaders of nations too. Duterte, the Philippine president, does this effortlessly. In one fell swoop, this once obscure mayor rose into power simply by touching a chord in the hearts of a desperate nation. No other national leader in history ever came to be due to the insistent pleadings of his people.*

This, my friend, is the height of inspiration—the art of people following you, not because they have to but because they want to.

4. Great leadership backs words with action

Jesus did not just teach. He walked the talk. When he said there's no greater love than giving one's life for a friend, he went ahead and died for them. In effect, his followers also chose to die for him when the occasion called for it because he made himself their friend. You don't have to go to the extent of dying for your followers but as a leader, you have to match your words and expectations you have of them with your action. If you set certain rules, you should be the first to comply with them—no matter how difficult. How do you expect your people to follow your rules if you are the first to break them? You know how children close their ears to instruction but open their eyes to example? It's the same thing for a leader's employees or followers.

A leader's every move is scrutinized, so behave in the same way that you expect your people to. If you advocate promptness and hard work, you should be the first to arrive and last to leave the office. If you are driving your people to conquer the market, you should be the first to invade the field.

As Mahatma Gandhi aptly said: "Be the change that you wish to see in the world."

5. Great leadership delivers

When Jesus said he would come back from the dead in three days, he delivered ahead of time. Because he fulfilled a seemingly impossible promise, his adherents' faith was steadfastly sustained by another promise—he would come again. Well, bringing one's self back to life is a hard act to follow—literally. In Jesus' case, he did not make a promise he couldn't fulfill, even if that meant braving the gates of hell. If you don't do this, you will not be taken seriously—take many politicians, for example. They most often over-promise and under-deliver. But when Duterte promised the war on drugs would be a bloody one, he quickly delivered more than 7,000 bodies in under a year. This is not to say his means of achieving his goals were right (though a majority of Filipinos supported it), but he sure made a hell of an effort to deliver on his promises at the cost of being condemned by the world.

As a leader, great things are expected of you, sometimes even impossible things. When you assume leadership, you make unspoken promises in the form of high expectations. A leader is expected to set the organization to the right direction, lead the people effectively, and bring them to the Promised Land. In the business arena, you make explicit promises to your people, to your customers, business partners, stakeholders, and to the public.

A promise is a commitment; fulfill your business commitments consistently and you will be able to breed a reliable workforce borne out of promised-based leadership.

If your people perceive you as someone who makes good on his promises – no matter what – you can be assured that they will stick by your side through thick and thin, and continually hope to see the fulfillment of the rest of your promises.

6. Great leadership keeps hope alive

When Jesus was resurrected, he demonstrated how even the most hopeless being could find hope. If he died and could rise up, anyone can rise up from adversity and difficult circumstances.

Lee Kuan Yew did this for Singapore, Steve Jobs for Apple, Elon Musk for Tesla, Warren Buffett for Berkshire Hathaway, and Lou Gerstner for IBM, and these are just a handful of examples. Hope is holding on to probabilities even at the worst of circumstances. Even when business is bad and things don't seem to be getting better, a leader must continue to make a positive impact in the lives of his followers. People need to believe in something. During one of the most severe setbacks in the history of the Philippines, Duterte sold hope to his people and they bought it. He inspired a powerful online and offline movement of desperate people who were hoping for a better life.

MAKING IT HAPPEN!

> *When your people have difficulties in their careers or
> even in their private lives, they need a harbinger of hope.*

Sometimes a leader has to tell their followers "everything's going to work just fine," if only to reconnect with a time of better circumstances.

7. Great leadership empowers

Ever wondered why followers of Jesus seem to continue to perform miracles of healing even in the 21st Century? It's not that Christian ministers are miracle workers. Rather, it is because Jesus empowered his believers to heal themselves through the power of their faith. In almost all of his healing sessions, Jesus did not claim credit for his accomplishments. Instead, he told those he healed "your faith has healed you." Thus, even to this day, anyone who believes without a doubt receives healing when it's asked for. Or their belief reveals prayers have been answered. They may not be aware of it, but their absolute belief (mental power) brought them the circumstances they asked for, simply because they received the authority to do so and they accepted it. Few people understand if a leader transfers his authority to those he leads, he is multiplied and empowered even more.

> *Great leaders pass the energy and credit to their people, empowering
> them with a new sense of direction and confidence in achieving it.
> Strong leaders believe in the capacity of their people to
> take responsibility and give them the authority to do so.
> They are responsive to the needs of their people and involve their
> followers in designing the future of their company.*

If you treat your employees as valuable partners and vital contributors to the success of your business, they will also treat your customers the same way. Empowering your people will give them the burning desire to accomplish great things for your organization.

8. Great leadership is willing to sacrifice

Jesus not only passed the credit on. He also took the blame. So much so that it is written about how he paid for the sins of men with his own life. No one has to go to that extent, but sacrifice is in the heart of leadership and Jesus perfectly demonstrated it. In return, he earned the undying love of his followers.

As a leader, you are expected to sacrifice your time, energy, money, and even your comfort so that those you lead may prosper and be safe. If your people perceive that you are willing to forgo your interests in their behalf, you will earn their love and loyalty—a very precious resource in your hands.

Love is the most powerful force in the universe. It has the power to change people and make them more responsive, positive, optimistic, resilient, tenacious, healthier, happier, and productive.

Loyal employees are exceptionally committed to their work and are willing to scale mountains just to please you. Imagine what that could do within the workings of your business.

Now you know how to be FIRST. Go and be the great leader that you really are.

"If anyone wants to be first, he must be the last of all and the servant of all."
— **Jesus of Nazareth**

MAKING IT HAPPEN!

7 | The Power of Negotiation

"In business as in life, you don't get what you deserve, you get what you negotiate."
— **Dr. Cet Karrass**

Life is a precarious balance of winning and losing, victory and defeat, failure and success. More often than anyone dares admit, the deciding factor between these opposing forces is the power to negotiate.

Without question, the world – as we see it today – is a product of failed and successful negotiations. That may sound like an overstatement but it's true. Successful negotiations can avoid war and uphold peace; save dying companies and create mergers; tear down walls and build bridges; preserve marriages and foster relationships; resolve conflicts and forge alliances. You see it in the market, when buyers and sellers haggle for the best deal. You see it in the courts, where lawyers offer to make a settlement, in the workplace, when employees ask for a raise, or between hostage-takers and professional hostage negotiators, where success or failure can either spell life or death.

If the negotiations between President Roosevelt and Prime Minister Fumimaro Konoye of Japan pushed through successfully, World War II would have been averted. Before the Pearl Harbor bombing, Prime Minister Konoye sent word to Washington through Ambassador Grew that he wanted to meet with President Roosevelt face-to-face in Honolulu, Hawaii in order to present his terms for a settlement. That was the only hope to turn around the situation at that time before it was too late. Roosevelt, however, wanted to include the British, the Chinese, and the Dutch allies in the discussion. Konoye insisted to meet with Roosevelt alone because he feared for his life. There were fanatical Japanese elements at that time who opposed any Japanese accommodation with the US. If the meeting was leaked to them, by chance, there was danger that Konoye would be assassinated. Konoye's rationale was that if he would meet with Roosevelt in Hawaii, accompanied by senior representatives of Japan's army and navy, the citizens' reaction and approval would override the fanatics' sentiments. Part of the August 18 cable sent by Ambassador Grew to Washington read:

"The Ambassador urges with all the force at his command for the sake of avoiding the obviously growing possibility of an utterly futile war between Japan and the United States that this Japanese proposal not be turned aside without very prayerful consideration....The good which may flow from a meeting Prince Konoye and President Roosevelt is incalculable. The opportunity is here presented, the Ambassador ventures to believe, for an act of the highest statesmanship, such as the recent meeting of President Roosevelt with Prime Minister Churchill at sea, with the possible overcoming thereby of apparently insurmountable obstacles to peace hereafter in the Pacific."[1]

It took so long for Washington to decide on the matter that Konoye lost hope of averting a war. He ultimately gave up on the proposed meeting and resigned. During October and November that year, Ambassador Grew sent several cables to Washington warning how the Japanese may resort to national Hara-Kari (honorable suicide) in order to free Japan from the freeze and embargo sanctioned by the allies.

On December 7, 1941, Japan bombed Pearl Harbor, killing 2,403 Americans.

On August 6 and 9, 1945, the US dropped the atomic bomb on Nagasaki and Hiroshima, killing 129,000 people, most of them civilians.

---

1 Amanda Watts. Joseph Grew and American-Japanese Diplomacy Leading to Pearl Harbor. Wesleyan University, Constructing the Past, Volume 15, Issue 1, 2014. Retrieved from https://digitalcommons.iwu.edu/cgi/viewcontent.cgi?article=1217&context=constructing.

The same is true to this very day. Our lives hang in balance as we are at the mercy of our leaders' mental attitudes. Some recognize this, but the number is far too few. We all need to be aware of this and better understand the power of negotiation.

The Art of Negotiation

The value of negotiation is not being emphasized enough, but in truth, it is more vital than war strategies. As the adage goes: an ounce of prevention is better than a pound of cure. In the world of business, the inability to negotiate will lead to others getting the lion's share and you being left with the crumbs.

You may not be aware of it, but you are involved in a series of negotiations daily. Do you remember the last time you were involved in a negotiation? Maybe not, because you didn't view it as such. Plus, negotiations are often conceived in terms of significant events such as averting a war, resolving a hostage conflict, facilitating a business merger, or discussing nuclear options. In truth, whether you are in the Oval Office or in the privacy of your bedroom, you negotiate every single day. At home, you negotiate about who does the dishes and who mows the lawn, who picks up the trash and who does the laundry, who pays the bills and who goes to the grocery store.

Outside, you negotiate with friends about what to do on weekends and where to spend the night; whether to paint the town red or white. At work, you negotiate for a salary raise, job assignments, or better benefits. The only difference is we go through life's daily negotiations effortlessly and without much thought, while we sweat and stammer when faced with huge issues.

The stakes are higher when it comes to big negotiations, but if you are mindful of the small ones and learning from them, you will have no problem tackling big issues.

Remember this: whether you are at the negotiating table or the kitchen table; whether the subject is crucial or petty, you employ the same tactics and skills.

When you were a kid, you were a shrewd negotiator. Remember when your Mom told you it's time for bed and you say "My friend doesn't go to bed until..." Or, you are told to turn the TV off and you say "twenty minutes more." You always knew how to get around certain situations and you seemed to get your way all the time, even when your parents had the upper hand and they could have easily bludgeoned you into obedience. Why were you such a hell of a negotiator back then? The answer is simple. As a child, you saw the power that adults wield.

Adults have the freedom to do what they want. No one tells them what to do (that children usually see) and they appear self-reliant. As a child, you wanted to be like them. You wanted power too—you wanted to be heard, you wanted to prove you were right and everyone else was wrong. You hated authority, you wanted control of the situation, so as much as possible you argued and negotiated. And you knew exactly how to win. You used your charms, sweetness, and strengths to get what you wanted. You were doing this in much the same way that successful, high-powered negotiators often do.

8 Tips for Remembering Your Negotiation Skills

"Look into the eyes of a child and you will find yourself face-to-face with one of the world's greatest negotiators."
— **Bill Adler, Jr.**

That fearless and confident child still exists in you. Let's touch base with what part of you felt like then, so you can hopefully resurface it for today's world.

1. You aimed for the stars

When you asked for candy, you always ask for more, right? You knew if you asked for two, you would get one, so you would ask for five. Even though you knew deep inside Mom would never agree to five, it was at least a good place to start. The same thing applies in the real world. Negotiation is all about the "room" and the flow of discussion. About pushing forward and back. It's like flying a kite. You don't want to pull too close because that will not let the kite fly. But at the same time, you don't want to let it go too far for fear that the line might snap and you might lose the entire kite. So the most effective way to negotiate is to start slightly higher than your actual asking. Plus, who knows…you might really end up with what you ask for, right?

"In business as in life, you don't get what you deserve, you get what you negotiate."
— **Chester L. Karrass**

Asking for a high price can give you a lot of room to negotiate. It's also an indication that you are not willing to settle for a lot less. As a rule, you might end up getting more if you ask for more.

2. You knew no limits

In your magical childhood world, all you had to do was ask and it appeared. In time, you realized that you had to negotiate to get more. Remember that wide-eyed expectation you used to have when you ask your mom for one more serving of dessert? You would ask without fear or hesitation, even offer to forego ice cream for one more cookie (you knew how to charm your way to a cup of ice cream later anyway). You were so confident and optimistic then. Through the years, the failures and rejections you experienced may have weakened your resolve, so now you often come to the bargaining table with less courage to ask for more. You've surrendered your negotiating power. This is where attitude comes in.

Attitude is an important part of the negotiation process. Today, it's already a well-accepted fact that your thoughts can influence your reality in a significant way. This is not new news. The principle is at least 2,000 years old and today it's being revived to adapt to today's social and business environment. "I tell you, you can pray for anything, and if you believe that you've received it, it will be yours," said the Teacher. Nothing can be more positive and optimistic than believing you have already received what you have asked for.

You need to believe in yourself once again in order to get the deal you want. You have more negotiating power than you think, so turn the positivity button on! Remember, optimism is a choice you make.

3. You knew how to add and trade value

Do you recall when you wanted your parents to buy you something expensive? You would be especially helpful around the house, surprisingly obedient and agreeable, and even give them a butterfly massage with your cute little fingers! You were going to get that new bike no matter what! The same principle works in business.

With business, if you have built a good reputation or done a favor for the other party, you already have an advantage. When Andrew Carnegie wanted to sell his steel rails to the Pennsylvania Railroad, he not only negotiated with J. Edgar Thomson (the president of Pennsylvania Railroad, he went beyond the norms by setting up a giant steel mill in the state and had it named "J. Edgar Thomson Steel Works." If you were Thomson, where would you buy your steel rails? The place without your name? Likely not! You may not be able to pull off a Carnegie, but you can still apply the same principle.

Make the other party feel important – even loved – and you will negotiate your way to success.

4. You mastered the art of timing

As a child, you instinctually understood perfect timing. You knew when to stand back and when to strike. You were a cute little kid that knew if Mom or Dad were in a bad mood, you'd definitely get a no, so you always waited for the right moment.

Dinnertime is often the right time for kids to ask for what they want. The conversation was pleasant, everyone was relaxed, no one was hungry, Mom and Dad were playful… Your chances of success were greater.

At the bargaining table, perfect timing is also important. If you buy a car, you can negotiate better terms when the office is about to close or at the end of the month—the time when salesmen and managers are scrambling to reach their quota. Black Friday deals can also save you thousands of dollars since it's the time to clear out older inventories for the New Year, not to mention the demand/desire to meet their quota. You'll also get an even greater bargain if the model is on the way out and dealers are eager to get new inventory in.

Do you remember who Ronald Wayne is? Far too few people remember him. He is the Apple founder and he chose the worst time to sell his 10% share of the company. He earned $800.00. Today, his shares would have been worth $53.8 billion. He lost the opportunity of a lifetime because of bad timing.

From wet markets to ornate boardrooms, timing is the difference between a botched deal and a lucrative one.

5. You knew how to play one side against another

As a kid, you knew that a "no" from Dad didn't equate to a "no" from Mom, and vice versa. So, what did you do when you didn't get a "yes" from one of them? You approached the other. And if that didn't work, you could be sure that Grandma could help and make an emotional appeal on your behalf while you smile mischievously behind her skirt. "Okay, just this once," your mother would reluctantly say. It was masterful, according to your young mind.

In the art of negotiation, you must know how to use your knowledge about the other party's positions and interests. A clever negotiator never fails to have an ace up their sleeve and use it when necessary.

6. You were a real charmer
Gone are the days when you only had to bat your eyes to draw Mom in. You were so freaking cute and adorable then; Mom couldn't spit out a "no" if she tried—even to your most unreasonable requests. But do you know you can become cute and adorable once again, this time, in the eyes of your business associates?

Being charming means being able to forget about yourself. When you were a kid, you got all the attention because you were adorable; now you can only be adorable if you don't draw attention to yourself. Charm is all about being genuinely interested in others; allowing them to talk about themselves, listening to them enthusiastically, complimenting them when the occasion calls for it, retaining eye contact, asking more questions about them, and most of all, uttering the sweetest sound in the world: their name. There is power in hearing your name!

This really comes together when they begin to ask you questions in return. Charm means being able to answer briefly, humbly, and agreeably. Let's face it. They are not interested to know the details of your vacation or your divorce—all they really care about is their own selves. So take note of every little detail they have told you and the next time you meet, ask them about their vacation in Boracay or about the new baby.

If you make people feel important and you genuinely care for them, you will become the most adorable business associate who will always have the upper hand on the negotiating table.

7. You always came prepared
Before you asked your parents to buy you the latest gadget, you already visited the store several times, memorized every intricate detail and feature, even dreamed about it day and night. Then you spent several days doing extra chores, being especially sweet and charming—you know, doing all those things that have proven themselves to work. You even rehearsed your lines! Then you mustered all your strength to finally stage the attack: "You have to buy that cellphone for me, everyone in school has one!" "My friends also have Lambo's. Does it mean I also

need to get one?" your Dad would try to dodge. "But Dad, how else can you track me if I'm lost or have an emergency?" Brilliant. In every negotiation, preparation and communication are critical. Know what you want to achieve and what you're prepared to take; what to give up and what to hold on to; what you're willing to compromise and what to fight for.

When you are prepared, you always know how to best present your case in a clear and concise manner, while also listening to the needs of the other party so you can use that to your advantage.

8. You won't take no for an answer

When you were a kid, the word "no" wasn't actually a "no" to you. You always knew how to turn things around. You insisted, pleaded, begged, negotiated, bargained, went on hunger strikes, threw a fit (when required), or sought out someone who could change your parents' minds. You were always on the lookout for the right strategy that would work so you could get what you wanted.

This "childish" trait used to be viewed negatively, but in reality, this is tenacity in action. Everybody knows the inspiring story of Colonel Harland Davis Sanders who had to cook his now famous Kentucky Fried Chicken on the spot for 1,009 restaurants before he could find someone who was willing to sell his chicken. As of 2017, the total KFC restaurants all over the world has reached 21,487 and still counting. His resilience paid off.

All the charm, strategy, cunning, manipulation, tactics, and optimism you can employ do not guarantee a 100% success in getting the deal you want all the time. Great news is, you can always take the offer to another table and improve on your skills every time.

Yes, the goal of negotiation is to get the best deal for your interests, but the real deal comes from finding an agreement to maximize the benefits and minimize the losses for both parties. If the other party walks out with a sense of fairness to them, you are a consummate negotiator.

MAKING IT HAPPEN!

Make an Impact

Remember, the result of a negotiation can greatly impact your future dealings and your business reputation. In addition to your innate negotiation skills, you can learn a thing or two from Andrew Carnegie's brilliant negotiation skills. In the 1850s, Andrew Carnegie monopolized the steel market. His company, the Central Transportation Company, supplied the steel used to build the railways connecting the United States. His happy days were short-lived though. George Pullman built his own steel manufacturing company and gave Carnegie a run for his money by offering his product at a much lower price. Carnegie responded by cutting his prices to beat the competition. Pullman would again lower his price and Carnegie would respond accordingly, until they were both losing and were on the verge of bankruptcy.

One day, in a twist of fate, Carnegie and Pullman were stuck in an elevator after a transport meeting and this gave Carnegie the opportunity to open his mind to Pullman. "We sure must both be the most foolish people on the planet," Carnegie suddenly spoke to a startled Pullman. There and then, Carnegie suggested a merger, where both of them could work together and operate profitably once again. When the hesitant Pullman asked Carnegie what would be the name of the new company, Carnegie answered without hesitation "Why, the Pullman Transportation Company, of course". Pure genius.

Great negotiation skills can spell the difference between losing altogether and a beneficial outcome.

While the amateur negotiator focuses only on getting what he wants, the ultimate negotiator considers the needs of his counterpart and looks for a win-win solution. The aim of a negotiation is to find a mutually acceptable solution for both parties. Dwight Eisenhower's father nailed it when he taught his son: "You must never try to make all the money that's in a deal. Let the other fellow make some money too, because if you have a reputation for always making money, you won't have many deals."

I negotiate on a daily basis for my work. Sometimes, I have to negotiate with my subcontractor for them to charge a lower fee. Sometimes I have to negotiate with the guy who gives me the project to work on to pay me more. But there was one particular negotiation I remembered which may remain my most important one to date.

I was working for Tom Shapiro for quite awhile before I decided I wanted to come out on my own. When I told him about the plan of me setting my own company and for him to engage me as a subcontractor instead of working as his employee, he wasn't excited at first. From his standpoint, why would I want to pay someone more to do the same work? But eventually I gave him a value proposition. I knew he always had a lack of manpower. I could fill that gap by providing him with it. I told him he would never have to worry for shortage of workers.

Once he understood letting me go and then re-engaging me as a subcontractor was profitable to him, while also saving him time and effort, he became keener on the idea. And because of that transition, I was able to earn more and hire more, eventually leading up to this point where I am able to chase after my dreams. I can put money in the bank, take time off to write and publish this book, and so on. In any other situation, this would have been impossible.

Now you're equipped with the best negotiation strategies; you know you can devour your counterpart hands down.

Let this wise saying guide you.

Real power, after all, is knowing you can, but you don't.

"The first rule of negotiation: be prepared to destroy the other side... and choose not to."
— **Dave Logan, Ph.D.**

MAKING IT HAPPEN!

8 | How to Live Healthy

"Health is a state of complete harmony of the body, mind and spirit. When one is free from physical disabilities and mental distractions, the gates of the soul open."
— **B.K.S. Iyengar**

This chapter is going to approach the topic of health from all perspectives. In other words, we are going to cover the body, mind and spirit. Why? Because living healthy isn't just about a healthy body. And it isn't just about a healthy mindset. And it isn't just about the spiritual aspect of your life either…

It's all three.

When it comes down to it, if you are going to live a healthy life, all areas of your life need to be healthy—not just one or two. And technically, there could be a fourth aspect, relationships and your social life. When any one of the four aspects suffers, all suffer.

Why Live Healthy?

Why bother with living healthy? What difference does it really make? If you are struggling in life right now, it may seem like it will take too much effort. After all, it takes time to work out, extra money to eat right, and more time to do things like meditate. This is true, but the truth you need to understand is the benefits you get from exercising, eating right, and doing things like yoga and meditation far outweigh the time and money it costs. Actually, they can ensure you're as fit as possible, which can help you become more successful in all areas important to you.

For example, studies show meditating for just 15 minutes a day will make you more productive throughout your day. So, if you think you don't have time to meditate, think again! If you're still not convinced, consider the following benefits.

You'll Feel Better Now

The benefits of healthy living are immediate. Most of us can tell the difference between eating a McDonald's hamburger for dinner versus a healthy organic meal. And most of us feel immediate gratification after a nice walk, jog, or run. And you can tell whether you had the benefit of a good night's sleep the very next day.

These results are felt quickly, and they also lead up to long-term results such as a longer life! This is a good segue into the next reason: live better, age better.

You'll Live Better and Age Better

For most of us, as we age, we slow down. But the better we take care of our body, mind, and spirit, the longer we'll have to enjoy our healthy life.

Let's face it! Aging really sucks. And when you're young, you totally take it for granted. You don't think about how decisions you make could affect yourself in significant ways later on. So, do all you can to live a healthy life style so you can continue to be active in life. There is nothing quite as disappointing as waking up one day and realizing you can no longer play your favorite sport – or do things you love – because you didn't take care of your body well enough.

By taking care of your body, mind, spirit, and your social life, you'll prolong the "good ole days" for continued "good days" because you are still youthful in heart, mind, and spirit.

Just take care of yourself! The better you do so, the better your chances are of offsetting the ramifications of aging. You have nothing to lose and everything to gain. Think about these benefits of living a healthy life…

- Experience less pain
- Look better longer
- Be happier!
- Better self-esteem
- More self-confidence
- Better sex drive
- Live longer
- Accomplish more; do more

The benefits to living a healthy life style are numerous. We're going to offer you seven excellent and appealing benefits.

7 Steps to Living a Healthy Life

None of these steps may be a part of your life, as you know it, today. You are highly encouraged to take the time to implement them as much as possible. I challenge you to make following them the norm, not the exception.

Step 1: Get Plenty of Sleep

Research shows getting a good night sleep is essential to your health. The younger you are, the more sleep you need. But in general, adults need 7 to 9 hours of sleep a night, depending upon the person. When you sleep, your body regenerates itself.

MAKING IT HAPPEN!

According to the article, *Your Body Does Incredible Things When You Aren't Awake* by Laura Schocker[2] and shared via Huffington Post, there are a number of health related things that your body does such as:

- Tissues grow and are repaired
- The cardiovascular system is improved
- Hormones, such as the human growth hormone, are secreted
- The regulation of appetite hormones occurs which curbs hunger pain
- New pathways in the brain are created for memory and learning
- A consolidation of memories occurs
- A reduction of fears

And more…

Clearly, if you aren't getting enough sleep, your body is going to suffer. As a wise Benjamin Franklin used to say, "Early to bed, early to rise makes a man healthy, wealthy, and wise!"

Step 2: Eat Healthy Foods

Jack LaLanne was the godfather of fitness. He used to say that you wouldn't feed your dog a doughnut and a cup of coffee for breakfast. And yet, that's what you'll do to yourself!

And then we wonder why we don't feel good, we're over-weight, and look bad.

Certainly, to a large extent, you are what you eat. But some people take eating healthy to an extreme. Somewhere in the middle is a balance that will serve you well for the rest of your life.

---

[2] Schocker, Laura. Your Body Does Incredible Things When You Aren't Awake. Huffington Post. Wellness Blog. December 6, 2017. Retrieved from https://www.huffpost.com/entry/your-body-does-incredible_n_4914577.

People are different, right down to what our body's can handle. Some people are lactose intolerant, while others are not. Some get allergies consuming food with gluten, and others are perfectly fine. Some do well eating meat and others do not... Clearly, there is no "one perfect diet" to meet all peoples' needs. And this is why so many diets fail. Usually, the creator of a diet gets excellent results for themselves, they market it and try to force it onto others—but it does not work.

So what should you do? What diet should you follow?

First, follow your gut instinct. Do what seems best for you. In general, you should gravitate toward organic foods as much as possible and stay away from processed foods. Fruits are also healthy but usually should be consumed in lower quantities because of the high levels of fructose.

If you are drawn to beef, try eating grass-fed beef. It's much healthier than regular grain-fed cows. Grass-fed beef has:

- Less total fat
- More heart-healthy omega-3 fatty acids
- More conjugated linoleic acid, a type of fat that's thought to reduce heart disease and cancer risks
- More antioxidant vitamins, such as vitamin E

As a side-point, losing weight is simpler than you may think. It's all about burning more calories than you are consuming. And one of the easiest ways to lose weight is to follow Dr. Mercola's unusual recommendation.

He says one of the best ways to lose weight is to teach your body to do incremental fasting. This is a technique where you teach your body to burn fat by skipping breakfast. If you are someone not hungry in the morning, this is great, but many people enjoy their breakfast, which means this seems painful! But the good news is you can train your body to skip breakfast.

MAKING IT HAPPEN!

How?

Simply eat breakfast a little later every day. Eat breakfast a half hour later every day for a couple weeks and before you know it, it will be the afternoon.

When you skip breakfast over time, your body will give up expecting food in the morning and instead, resort to burning fat. And when it starts to burn the fat in the morning, you'll lose weight easily and quickly.

Again, Dr. Mercola's method has worked for many. You still need to rely on your own intuition when it comes to eating. No matter what process you try, make it your goal to eat as much "live" food as possible, and eat as natural and as organic as you can.

If you use your own judgment and intuition, you can't go wrong.

Step 3: Exercise

According to the godfather of fitness Jack LaLanne, exercise is the most important thing that you can do for your body. He believed in good nutrition too, but exercise came first.

He also used to say that the best exercise to live longer, stay in shape and to look your best was working out with weights. He even invented exercise machines like the lat pull down, the leg extension, and the leg curl. These exercise machines are still used in gyms today.

But the truth is any exercise that gets the heart pumping is good for you. There are many types of beneficial exercise such as running, jogging, walking, swimming, or playing any sport.

Even golf is good for older ones who cannot play the more intense sports like basketball and football. Just keep in mind that as age sets in, flexibility tends to be lost. So, it's also a good idea to develop a good stretching routine.

Having said that, yoga is a good choice and it doesn't necessarily raise the heart rate much, but is very good for you. It strengthens, tones, and keeps the body flexible.

Swimming is an excellent for older individuals because it is easy on the joints. Actually, it's one of the best forms of exercise *for all of us.*

It is best if you can find something you really enjoy. This way, you are more likely to do it regularly. And if you can find a partner to do it with, this is all the better. When someone else is depending upon you, you're more likely to stick to your commitment.

As far as frequency is concerned, all the experts suggest you should exercise at least 3 to 5 times a week for at least 30 minutes. But it does depend upon what your goals are. Of course, if you want to lose weight, you may need more exercise than this.

Think of your body as your temple. You only have one, and you have to take care of it in order to get the most out of life. Although exercise may seem like too much effort, it is a critical component in order to live a healthy life.

And the truth is that once you develop a good habit of exercising, you'll look forward to it more and want to do it.

But in order to live healthy, taking care of your body is only one component. In addition, you must take care of your mind and spirit too.

Let's cover that next.

Step 4: Meditate

According to the late Dr. Wayne Dyer, all of us have about 60,000 thoughts per day, and most of those thoughts are not good ones. This is why meditation is good—it helps us to stop our thoughts, relax, and rejuvenate.

MAKING IT HAPPEN!

Meditation reduces stress, improves concentration, encourages a healthy lifestyle, increases self-awareness, increases happiness, slows aging, and benefits the cardiovascular and immune health.

- It is a great way to start your day and to remove any stress and anxiety that you may have in your life.
- You only need to meditate between 15 to 20 minutes a day so it's not very time consuming.

You may be thinking that meditation is not for you—you don't quite get it and you don't think you'd benefit. You may not "think" you'll benefit, but if you commit to it, it's as close to a guarantee as you can get that you'll "feel" its benefits.

The reason why it may not seem very beneficial could be you simply haven't really given it enough time. The good news is the benefits of mediation are cumulative, meaning the longer you do it (the number of different times), the better the results.

The other reason you may not like to meditate is because of how you were doing it. And although any type of meditation is better than nothing, the instructions below may help you to enjoy your meditation sessions more. In either case, it would be a good idea to give meditation another chance in order to live a healthy life.

- Locate a timer, perhaps an eye mask, some white noise (for focus), and a comfortable chair to sit in. Don't lie down because it is way too easy to fall asleep—sleep is great, but it's not meditation. When you're awake, you're giving your conscious mind the opportunity to relax and de-stress.
- Find a place where you can sit in your comfortable chair in a darkened room. You can make the room darker or you could wear the eye mask.
- During the meditation, you're going to need to find something to listen to like a ticking clock (the white noise). If you don't have one, you could listen to the hum of a fan, or an air conditioner. What you are attempting to do is to listen to something that will distract you from

your own thoughts, but not be too distracting or interesting to listen to. This is why a ticking clock, a fan, an air conditioner, or any repetitive, boring sound is good.

- Once you are ready, turn the timer on and sit in your chair.

- Close your eyes and begin by FOCUSING on the repetitive sound of your choosing. The goal here is to stop thinking. When you stop thinking, you stop the worry and the stress.

- When you have a thought come in, treat it like it is a float in a parade and you are there to watch it float on by. Don't try to stop it—just observe it, let it go, and don't give it any more attention. Your mind is a thought creation machine. So, to suddenly attempt to stop thinking is not really possible.

- As you meditate, listening to the repetitive, boring sound, you may get the urge to move or scratch. It's fine to itch if it's distracting, but ideally, you want to be still.

- If your mind is just too active, another option to help you to stop your thoughts is to repeat a "mantra." A mantra is just a word or phrase to help you keep other thoughts from coming. Your mantra could be something like, "relax," or "all is well," or something else that suits you. You could try doing the mantra for a little while, then listening to the repetitive sound again. And if you start to think too many thoughts again, then go back to your mantra. Over time, you won't have to do the mantra anymore because you will have trained your mind to stop your thoughts. Then you can solely listen to the repetitive sound.

- You know that you are doing it right when you start to feel like your arms and legs have disappeared! The feeling is very strange at first and you may think that something is wrong. But it's not. This simply means it's working. Some meditation gurus say what happens is when you get that sensation, it means you are connecting more fully with your "soul," higher self, or inner being.

MAKING IT HAPPEN!

*When you just go with the flow and enjoy it, it's a wonderful feeling.
Some describe it as blissful and peaceful.
It can also feel like you're in ecstasy.*

- If your body starts to sway or move, that's totally normal too. You may feel like it's not you even doing it! But don't worry—you have full and complete control. You can come out of meditation any time that you like.

- Once the timer goes off, slowly come back to the room.

That's it! That's all there is to it.

After about 21 days of meditating every day, it will become a habit for most people. Some people take less time, some longer. Once you develop it as a good habit, you'll never want to stop.

Step 5: Appreciate Something!

One of the keys to living healthy is having a positive attitude. When you have a positive attitude, all components of YOU are helped. In other words, your body, mind, and spirit are nurtured.

Even if things are really bad in your life, there is always something you can appreciate. You can appreciate the abundance of air, your healthy body, the roof over your head, a meal, a stranger, a sunset, an animal—anything around you, large or small, is a potential source of appreciation. Few things beat an appreciative heart. It leads to a positive outlook and attitude about life—which is a key to living a healthy, vibrant, and happy life.

Step 6: Create a Vibrant Social Life

We are social creatures. And we are happier and feel more fulfilled when we have a vibrant, active social life. So, from a practical standpoint, this means we do our best to keep our old friends, while also being open to new friendships. Relationships help us grow in many ways.

However, many times we outgrow old friends and need to move on. Sometimes, our friends mean well, but they can drag us down. They may be too negative, not understand our growth goals and desires, or just be envious of where we want to head compared to where they feel they are moving. If this is the case for you—it is best to let them go.

Saying you need a social life is one thing and pursuing an active, vibrant social life can be quite the other! You can take advantage of one of the many social media websites like www.meetup.com, where you can meet people who have the same interests.

There is nothing quite like a good friendship to enhance your health and life. Go ahead and find your tribe.

Step 7: Live Your Purpose

There is a saying by the late Dr. Wayne Dyer that goes, "Don't die with your music still in you." What he meant by this is life is too short to not pursue your dreams. At some point – sooner, rather than later – consider taking steps toward doing what you long to do, not just what you feel obligated to do.

According to a Gallup poll[3], 85% of people hate their jobs, especially their bosses! Do you really want to live your entire life doing work that you hate? What kind of a life is that?

The problem is compounded by the fact that companies are not nearly as loyal to their employees as they used to be. So, the argument that you have to stick to your job because of security is not as true as it used to be.

Dare to be yourself…

Dare to follow your heart…

---

3 Burrows, Sara. 85% of People Hate Their Jobs, Gallup Poll Says. Return to Now. September 22, 2017. Retrieved from https://returntonow.net/2017/09/22/85-people-hate-jobs-gallup-poll-says/.

MAKING IT HAPPEN!

Dare to start your own business…

Of course, do it in a rational way. It's never a good idea to suddenly jump ship from work and then try to start a business. You've already learned all about that in the chapter about starting a business. As a reminder:

The best way to start a business is to work part-time on your dream, and then when you launch and begin to make as much money as you do with your "other" job, you can quit.

It's really that simple… The world needs more entrepreneurs! For every desire, passion, and want out there, there is a business in the making. And nowadays, with the internet, you can make a lot of money doing what you want to do.

There are many YouTube channels where people are making a killing doing what they love. So can you! It takes time, energy, and work to get anything going: get rich quick methods don't really exist. But when you do what you love, you will have the desire to make it through the tough times every business has.

And being your own boss and achieving your dreams is an exciting form of health that is good for you mentally and physically. It's invigorating and keeps you alert and attuned to the pulse of the world. Enjoy these benefits!

Overall Health

Living a healthy life isn't just about your body. It isn't just about your mind and spirit either. It's about all three, plus having a social life. And when you balance all these aspects out, you are making sure you live a happier life. You are making it happen!

About Mario J. Muthe

Mario J. Muthe was born in Hidalgo, Mexico. Being the oldest of three siblings, he assumed the role of breadwinner at a very young age. In December of 1993, at the mere age of fifteen, he decided there was more to the world and he wanted to see it. Mario decided to pursue the American dream. Coming from a family below the poverty line, Mario borrowed some money in order to finance his move to the United States.

Mario arrived in America as a complete stranger, without knowing a single word in English. His only labor option was manual labor. He began working on rural farms, picking strawberries, tomatoes, and tobacco. This struggle lasted for two years. Understanding the importance of English, he decided to start taking English classes. He would travel to churches and learning centers where they would provide free classes. While he worked, he practiced his English. Once he was proficient, he then began working as a construction worker. Working his way from the bottom, he consistently invested in his own skills and remained dedicated at his work. He knew investing in himself was his pathway to creating a new future—not just for him, but also for his family and kids.

After years of struggles, Mario has emerged as the true manifestation of the American dream. Now, at the age of forty, he is happily married with three children. He owns a very successful construction company. He is also a highly sought after personal development coach. After learning from top leaders around the world, he is now embarking on a new journey—to educate and motivate people who may be experiencing situations similar to what he has in their own lives. He wants to help them understand how hard work can make any dream turn into reality. It's a combination of sweat and mindset!

Contact Mario J. Muthe

Website:
www.mariomuthe.com

Facebook:
Mario J. Muthe - Making It Happen

Instagram:
@MarioJMuthe

www.ingramcontent.com/pod-product-compliance
Lightning Source LLC
Chambersburg PA
CBHW021436210526
45463CB00002B/530